EDUCATING CHILDREN FOR LIFE:

The Modern Learning Community

by
Annemarie Roeper

Trillium Press
Monroe, New York

DEDICATION

I would like to dedicate this book to the children of the world and in particular to the children of Roeper City and Country School and those children I have met in California. All of them are my inspiration.

Copyright © 1990, Trillium Press, Inc.
All Rights Reserved.

Trillium Press, Inc.
PO Box 209
Monroe, NY 10950
(914) 783-2999
Fax (914) 782-6359

Trillium Press
203 College St., Suite 200
Toronto, Ontario
M5T 1P9 Canada

ISBN: 0-89824-198-7
Printed in the United States of America by the Royal Fireworks Press of Monroe, New York.

TABLE OF CONTENTS

Acknowledgment	iv
Preface	vi
Introduction	1
The Dilemma of Modern Education	3
A Philosophy of Self-Actualization and Interdependence	15
The Reality of the Self	23
The Development of Self: Viewing the Child From the Inside Out	27
The Self-Actualization, Interdependence Model	34
The Role of the Teacher in the SAI Model	37
The Role of the Teacher in Relation to the Group	41
Curriculum in the Self-Actualization, Interdependence Model	46
Rules and Behavioral Attitudes in the SAI Model	62
The Roeper City and Country School Experience	74
Appendix	97

ACKNOWLEDGMENT

This book is the result of living my life. All of my life experiences have been integrated into a conscious or unconscious pool of insights, beliefs, concepts and ideas which originate from a diversity of sources and have come together in a unified whole. This reservoir is the background for the book and, therefore, the book contains something from everyone who has played a major role throughout the years in my life and the life of the school.

The silent co-author of this book has been my husband, George. Next year we will celebrate our fiftieth anniversary. We have raised a family together, founded a school and conceptualized our life's philosophy; and yet became independent individuals who not only shared a vision, but learned from their relationship.

Our three children, Tom, Peter, and Karen, have been a special inspiration which is enhanced by the wisdom of my grandchildren, Maria and Jamey, and the sweetness of Tim. The educational philosophy of my parents, Drs. Max and Gertrude Bondy, and my childhood in their boarding school are the foundations of my approach to life and education. Richard and Editha Sterba, Viennese psychoanalysts, invited us to come to Detroit to take over the Editha Sterba Nursery School, which later became the Roeper City and Country School. The Sterbas became my personal and professional mentors.

There are a great number of people who have made an impact on the school and on our lives. There are so many members of our school community — coworkers, parents, board members and, in the profoundest sense, children — who are represented in this book. As I thought about ways to acknowledge this, an image appeared in my mind. It was as though a door to my mind opened and a person well-known and loved by me appeared. Soon another came, and then another, and then another until it became a crowd. It looked like a wonderful reunion. Each time a new person entered, it was clear that this particular person was really an integral part of my life and growth. Soon the room was filled and still they kept coming. I looked at each and knew they could not be left out of my acknowledgment. Yet, it became clear that each participant in my inner reunion could not possibly, appropriately be given the recognition she or he deserved. I was also concerned about anyone who could not make it to the reunion and yet belonged as much as everyone else. Therefore, I decided not to mention any names, but please feel personally appreciated.

This book also contains something from all my friends in many parts of the world. The gifted child movement and many of its representatives played a great role in my thinking. Elizabeth Drews comes to mind. She became a special friend with whom I had many inspiring conversations. Harry Passow assembled a group of experts in 1964 at our school to develop a program to form the basis for our school to become a school for the gifted. There is also Paul Brandwein who surrounds gifted education with a broad philosophical framework. My interests, friendships, study and work outside the school and since we moved to California include psychoanalysis, the women's movement. civil rights, and peace movements and the people who represent them and whom I have met are intertwined in this book. Again, I cannot begin to mention everyone.

Some of my greatest friends have been books and, through them, their authors. Books have been an enormous enrichment for my life and growth. They are not my possessions, but truly my friends. They have stimulated my thinking just as conversations with people have. They have included works by philosophers, psychologists, psychoanalysts, educators, politicians, artists as well as German and English fiction and fiction from other countries. I have spent much time thinking about a bibliography, but have felt very resistant to the thought because enumerating books and their authors would not reveal the reality of my relationship to them.

There are a number of people who have been specifically involved in making this book become a reality and who have given me a great deal of emotional and practical support over the years during which this book has been written. Sanford and Izora Cole originally encouraged me to write the book and planned to publish it, which, for a variety of reasons was not possible. My daughter-in-law, Laura Holland, read a part of the original version and made some very pertinent, constructive criticism. Discussions with Ina Schlessinger added new insights. Marjory Raskin always inspired me to think critically. Kay Peven was a tactful critic of some of my writing. Pam Blair inspired me with her research on children's fears and typed some of an early version of this book. Great support, which helped whenever I was ready to give up, came from Harry Passow who agreed to write an introduction. Tom Kemnitz consistently supported my efforts and waited patiently for me to finish. A turning point in my commitment to finish this book came when Connie Shannon spent a month with us and helped me formulate some basic concepts through gently asking the right questions. Linda Silverman did the most extraordinary job of editing, which included supportive remarks in almost every paragraph.

This book would have been discarded long ago if it had not been for Pat Hatchel who helped me with editing, careful corrections, and tactful criticism, as well as many typings and retypings.

This book would have never been written were it not for the many thoughtful, earnest, enthusiastic children whom I was able to observe in their efforts to find the best way to live in this complex world.

Many thanks to every one of you.

Annemarie Roeper

PREFACE BY A. HARRY PASSOW

It was in June 1956 that I first met Annemarie Roeper. At the invitation of Annemarie and George Roeper, I had arrived to spend a week at their City and Country School in Bloomfield Hills, Michigan, chairing a meeting that was to plan the "conversion" of the school to one for gifted children. I think there were about ten of us, including Annemarie and George, who spent that week together in what I still recall some 32 years later, as one of the most challenging, exciting activities I had ever been involved in.

Two years earlier, I had initiated the Talented Youth Project at Teachers College, Columbia University, and my colleagues and I had already designed and started to implement research and development in the field of the gifted. But, here we were being asked by the Roepers to design a school of our dreams! And dream we did that week as we explored every aspect of what a school for the gifted should be—from its guiding philosophy, to the selection of its students, to its curriculum design and instructional strategies, to its staffing, to its overall ethos and climate.

We made our plans—fully expecting that George and Annemarie would implement them, and we were not disappointed. The City and Country School became—and still is—a remarkable school with a program guided by a unique philosophy of what education should be. In retrospect, the reason that our advice to the Roepers during that week-long planning meeting in June 1956 was actually heeded and acted upon is quite simple: my colleagues and I re-invented what Annemarie and George Roeper had arrived at and believed in long before our discussions.

Annemarie Roeper has subtitled her book, *The Modern Learning Community,* because that is exactly what the Roepers aimed at and succeeded in creating in their school. She is not using hyperbole when she opens her acknowledgement observing that:

> This book is the result of living my life. All of my life experiences have been integrated into a conscious or unconscious pool of insights, beliefs, concepts and ideas which originate from a diversity of sources and have come together in a unified whole. This reservoir is the background for the book and, therefore, the book contains something from everyone I have encountered in my life.

Annemarie Roeper's purpose in writing this book is "to articulate an approach to education which goes beyond the concept of education and represents a philosophy of life, a philosophy which she and George spent their lifetime living, refining, and developing. This philosophy, as she puts it simply and elegantly, "is based on the belief of self-actualization, respecting the growth and uniqueness of the community as well as the reality of mutual interdependence...only becom[ing] a reality through its implementation." With the Roepers, this philosophy is not empty rhetoric; they have demonstrated that "it can be implemented by all who believe in it and understand it." That's what the Roeper City and Country School was and is all about.

Annemarie begins with an insightful discussion of what she calls "the dilemma of modern education" in order to provide the reader with a clear understanding of "where she is coming from." She then presents a philosophy of self-actualization and interdependence which represents a "philosophy of both learning and life." Readers will find this discussion of the philosophy and its implementation specific and meaningful, well-illustrated by examples taken from Annemarie's 40-plus years of reflective experience. What she means by "Self" and by self-actualization are made clear as well as the role of the teacher in nurturing the self, all amply illustrated with examples from the Roeper school. The ideas are provided in the form of a model—the Self-Actualization, Interdependence Model—with a goal of "educating children for life," providing "the learner with opportunities for total personality growth within the conceptual framework of all aspects of global interdependence." Annemarie examines the rationale, the content, the processes, the conceptual frameworks, drawing on the traditional areas to explicate how "the whole curriculum and learning environment are embedded and surrounded by a strong interdependent community where the child learns the basic skills and concepts of cooperation."

Annemarie Roeper has done, I think, a remarkable job of describing the essence of the Roeper City and Country School—its life, function, climate, relationships, governance, resource use—as these contribute to implementing the Self-Actualization Interdependence Model. While the school is known as a school for the gifted, readers will soon recognize that what Annemarie Roeper is advocating is appropriate for *all* children. The "cooperative, nonhierarchial philosophy and system of education" which is embodied in the Roeper School—the modern learning community—has meaning for *all* educators.

One can find all too few examples in the literature where insightful educators have distilled their life-long efforts to educate children and youth in a particular way toward a particular goal. Annemarie Roeper's text will be a welcome addition to this scarce genre.

A. Harry Passow
Jacob H Schiff Professor of Education
Teachers College, Columbia University

INTRODUCTION

The purpose of this book is to articulate an approach to education which differs fundamentally in philosophy and application from the conventional approach of traditional education. It is, in fact, based on a vision which goes beyond the concept of education and represents a philosophy of life. During the forty years my husband George and I were heads of the Roeper City and Country School, we were involved in living with this philosophy and implementing it. The result was a school with a strong, unique atmosphere apparent to visitors and members of the community alike. There have been many opportunities at which we have tried to put our concepts into words but have never succeeded completely. The reason was that even we ourselves saw our approach as only a modification of a universally accepted framework. Because these concepts had never been fully articulated, it appeared as though our personal style and personalities created the Roeper approach. Therefore, the only way to maintain this and insure its continuation was to build a future on the Roeper tradition. This belief did not seem to express our own vision, but rather contradicted it. It was only after our retirement that we finally realized that this educational approach represents a uniquely different principle, and, therefore, not a tradition tied to us as individuals.

This philosophy is based on the belief of self-actualization, respecting the growth and the uniqueness of each member of the community as well as the reality of mutual interdependence. This philosophy only becomes a reality through its implementation. It is valid if it permeates every aspect of the particular educational community, without exception. It is a concept of self-actualization for all, as opposed to the concept of education for outside success where the primary focus is on what one can do rather than who one is as a human being. I feel the urgency to describe this concept and show that it is universally applicable and can be implemented by all who believe in it and understand it.

I am convinced that the success model of traditional education has succeeded in developing people who are highly capable, but has failed in satisfying people's need for self-actualization and learning how to become participating members in an interdependent community. The unfulfilled need for self-actualization seeks fulfillment all through the life of the individual, and the result to date has been the inability of human beings to manage their affairs constructively and cooperatively. Therefore, the times demand a more universal application of the self-actualization interdependence philosophy.

This book will begin with a description of the dilemma of modern education and then continue with the three parts of the model based on the self-actualization philosophy of cooperation as we tried to implement it at the Roeper City and Country School. The first part will consider in more detail the philosophy and discuss the specific goals emerging from it. The second part will be a discussion of the "Self" and its emotional and developmental phases. The third part will be an indepth explanation of our approach as one of the ways to implement the philosophy, with examples of major areas in our particular educational community. These areas will include some description of learning environment, methods and strategies of learning, approaches to subject matter, the role of the adults, interaction of community members, and governmental and administrative structures.

The desire for cooperative existence and self-actualization has existed throughout the ages and has always been confronted with the more universally accepted concept of hierarchy. The community of Roeper City and Country School is not the only one to implement a cooperative, nonhierarchical philosophy and system of education. However, it is the one I am most familiar with; and I will often refer to it as an example.

THE DILEMMA OF MODERN EDUCATION

Humanity has made two promises to its children. The first is to prepare a world which accepts them and provides them with opportunities to live, grow and create in safety. The other is to help them develop their whole beings to the fullest in every respect. Education is the vehicle through which we try to keep these promises.

Any system of education consists of three basic components. The first sets forth the goals, the philosophy of education: What are we trying to achieve? Where are we trying to go? The second component examines the characteristics of those to be educated, in other words: Whom are we educating? What does the child bring to the educational process? How will this student use the educational situation? Out of these first two components grows the third: the process of education. How are we going to achieve the stated goals, given the characteristics of the student to be educated?

The various ways in which different educators have dealt with these components account for the development of an enormous diversity of systems which are often in contradiction to each other. It is impossible, and not part of my intent to describe or respond to them all. I would not be able to do justice to them. For the purpose of this chapter, I will speak only about the predominant concept of education, the one which affects and confronts the majority of children, the one which is generally considered the norm against which all others have to measure themselves, prove themselves and defend themselves. I want to emphasize that I am aware of the fact that what I am about to say does not apply to every educational institution.

Today, I see education in a continuing dilemma. It often seems as though education is blamed for all our nation's ills, despite the fact that education has always been the foundation of growth in this country and all over the world. Throughout history, ownership of literacy was more valuable in terms of power and opportunities than ownership of money and property. This is why slave owners did not want their slaves to learn to read. To withhold literacy was to retain power and opportunity.

In the early days, education was considered the path which would lead to the fulfillment of all dreams. In those days, the goal was clear and was not questioned by anyone. There was a concept of characteristics of children and how they learn, limited by the state of knowledge of psychology of the times. The motivation of the individual was strong. The process and content were appropriate. They were in tune with the child rearing methods of the time. Not only were other options unavailable, there was no recognition that any were needed. Education led to the good life.

In reality, education continued for a long time to be a privilege that was limited in availability and in scope. Then, as today, it brought much tragedy and disappointment. The strong commitment of society to education, combined with its concepts of child rearing methods, often led to enormous suffering for children, but it was the only door which lead to ever increasing opportunities. Due to this strong commitment, the United States is one of the few countries in the world where universal education has become a reality. We have made a great deal of progress in all areas, including educational programs and psychology. Why, then, do we witness a general disenchantment today that was not evident then? What has caused the present situation?

The success and failure of our educational system is a source of endless debate. I have witnessed the ebb and flow of new ideas and new approaches during the past forty years. During that time progressive education came and went. There was a return to a more traditional approach sparked by Russia's Sputnik. This, in turn, gave way to a wave of interest in the integrated day, or open classroom, a form of progressive education initiated in England. Then Back to Basics was expected to solve all problems forever. And still, education continues to be found wanting. The newspapers are filled with reports of low test results and lack of skills and information among our children, which are interpreted as failures of education. In addition, we hear about social problems, such as drug abuse, sex among young adolescents, delinquency, truancy, dropouts, vandalism, depression and suicide.

Society looks for the culprit in many places: permissive child rearing, mediocre teacher training, mediocre teachers, mediocre administrators, mass education, low teacher salaries, class size, or classroom conditions. We look for remedies by trying to change the conditions which society believes caused the problems. This results in increased pressure on children and teachers, more demands to conform, proposals of merit pay for teachers, more emphasis on skills, back to the three R's, etc. In many ways, we are unfair to our educational system in that we treat it like a doctor treating a patient's symptoms without taking the time and thought to determine and treat the underlying cause. We are fighting fires, but not addressing the conditions supporting combustion.

We need to look again at those promises we all want to keep. We need to look at all the components of education, not just individually in fragmented isolation, but in relation to each other as part of a whole. We need to determine the content of each component based on today and tomorrow, not in terms of yesterday or the way we would like it to be, but in terms of reality. We may even have to deal with the fact that there may be more than one "right" answer. We know there are several wrong answers.

EDUCATIONAL GOALS AND PHILOSOPHY:

Our educational goals and procedures were established more than a hundred years ago. They have existed in much the same manner ever since. This means the original reasons for their existence may no longer be valid. They are taken for granted and now exist just because they have always existed. They have become a tradition continued for its own sake, and there is an unspoken taboo which says this tradition may not be examined or changed. Thus the three components of education have been frozen in history. This, by its very nature, has established a gap between the facts of today's reality and the goals and methods of education.

We are now living in a world which is much more interdependent than was the case previously. This calls for a change in our approach to education. But because education is still based on tradition, this is not happening in a fundamental way. We are not looking at the purposes of modern education. We have not thought about why we are doing what we are doing. We have not established a philosophy which relates to modern life. We continue to educate for the next step, the next test, the next grade, the next school. We educate in isolated fragments, and we fail to bind the fragments together into a meaningful whole. We fail to ask the reason for doing each step; we are content to fulfill the expectations of the next step.

Not only are today's children living in a different world, they themselves have changed since traditional education became established, and so has our knowledge of children and education. Our understanding of child development has increased tremendously. Real awareness of modern conditions and modern child psychology necessitates a reevaluation of whom we are educating, of our goals, methods and procedures, of the skills, attitudes and concepts to be achieved. It is the tragedy of modern education that this reevaluation is not taking place.

There is not much emphasis on new definition of basic goals or development of a philosophy in our modern educational system. Instead, there are some ideas as to the why of education, much of it based on our old tradition, much of it caused by some realization of the necessary changes without an indepth look at them. Therefore, we are left with some vague concepts, hopes and notions of education, such as: we are doing what we have always done, or our parents and grandparents received the same type of education and they have done alright, or this traditional approach will make our children successful and enable them to reach the top, or to compete, or to do well economically, or to serve their country, to become our best resources, to understand the real world. It will equip them to be winners in such a world, to be popular, to be leaders.

There are also those who believe education will open the doors to enjoyment of beauty, to help others, to express our creativity, etc. Do we know that the existing method leads to those envisioned results? Do we have a realistic view of the modern world and what our children need to be and learn in order to live in it successfully and to thrive in the future?

Most parents and educators have little time to spend thinking about defining a philosophy, goals and purposes of education. Most of us are being overwhelmed by the complexities of life. We are struggling to be in charge of our lives and are finding little time and opportunity for developing clear-cut concepts for the future of our children. Even in most books about education, the space spent on philosophy may be only one or two pages, while the rest is on how and what to teach: content and process. The importance of the philosophy in determining the outcome of education does not seem to be fully recognized.

There are also those who have thought about a philosophy of life and education, thought about it thoroughly, but find it difficult to relate their philosophy to everyday living and everyday occurrences. I have heard beautiful speeches made at conventions by keynote speakers who expounded in generalities about what we ought to be striving for. And they sounded good and thoughtful. But they did not bridge the gap to reality. Often, these speeches would then be followed by sessions on curriculum and teaching strategies. These sessions would not reflect the philosophy expressed by the keynote speaker as an educational goal which should be integrated with our teaching. The same people who might have reacted with great enthusiasm to the keynote speech would not or could not see the lack of connection to other sessions or to their own approach to teaching.

Since in general we do not have a philosophy of life and education, education has proceeded without one. It has, therefore, become isolated and alienated from life. It has become based on narrow, short-term goals, which we somehow believe will fulfill mankind's promises. We believe existing methods of education will magically achieve our hopes for each of our children to lead a happy, healthy, successful life as s/he accumulates wealth and wisdom and to lead a life which will contribute to the improvement of the world. If s/he learns all the so-called basic skills and goes obediently and successfully through the system and enters a prestigious college, will s/he be happy, wealthy and wise? Or do we just assume that this will be the consequence? Have we ever examined the cause and effect of our educational processes realistically? Have we looked at the adults that our system has produced? Are they healthy, wealthy and wise? Are they using their full potential? Are they equipped to deal with modern life? I have not seen many efforts made to determine this. I think that we raise illiterates when it comes to mastering the science or art of living. I do not even believe that education encourages children to prepare for life in daily acts and thoughts. The conscious and existing goal has become much more limited. We are really engaged in preparation for college.

Education for college as the real goal creates many subgoals, each becoming even more limited in scope. These subgoals really become education for the next step. In kindergarten, we educate for the first grade or even for a specific first grade teacher. In elementary school we educate for high school, and in high school we educate for college. These are the goals that the majority of people accept uncritically as the basic philosophy of our educational institutions. Whatever is expected at each level is considered the norm, the way it is supposed to be, the step that somehow will miraculously lead all our children to the promised land. There is little evidence that this is really so, and no one has truly proven it to be so.

It is no wonder that along the way many students become disillusioned, drop out of school, or drop out of society altogether. Many experience a culture shock when they enter life as an adult in society, or try to enter the work force. They find they are not necessarily prepared to cope with either. Particularly the gifted, by the very nature of their characteristics and awareness, find it difficult to accept this state of affairs as a given. They are questioners, and they find that these goals are not the ones that they would like to pursue, nor do they find them to be promising in terms of happiness and ability to cope with life.

CHARACTERISTICS OF THE LEARNER:

The second component is the characteristics of those to be educated. Here also, I believe that we are basing our concepts on old realities and perceptions. I believe these assumptions are alienated from the real personality of the modern child and our modern knowledge of child psychology and developmental theory. We assume that all children learn in the same manner, that they are vessels to be filled, and therefore, the essential ingredient for learning is the activity of teaching rather than the activity of the child as learner and grower.

We also believe that a people somehow can be fractured into small pieces, that they can bring their minds to school and leave their emotions at home. Many teachers and administrators look at the emotional side or the emotional needs of children as a troublesome interference with their primary task. "Schools are for academics, not for emotions," is a slogan that I have heard many times. We forget that the child is one total person who receives all experiences against the same background—the child's "Self." The child acts and reacts accordingly in all situations.

Traditional education is based on the assumption that we shape children like clay, rather than that they grow and that they bring something to the situation, which will change the way in which they will receive our teaching. This assumption also grows out of the notion that all learning is cognitive, and that other parts of growth which in reality act upon and interact with any learning, such as creative expression, physical growth and emotions, are merely frills to be added when time is left over. They are not really considered as belonging in the classroom.

Because we ignore these factors which might contribute to a child's personality, we have never really been able to understand the motivation or the lack of motivation for academic learning. Our whole approach says to the child, "You are a passive recipient, not an active participant in your learning process." We do not examine whether that is truly human nature, and whether that is truly the way a child grows and learns. From this it also follows that we ignore the hidden curriculum, i.e., the consequences children draw from teachers' behaviors, from the structure of the institution, and from their peers and other experiences. We really believe that they will learn what we teach them, as we teach it, and only that. I think that the largest body of learning takes place outside of the curriculum and probably this type of learning has a more permanent and integrative impact on the child than that provided by the curriculum.

The concept of the child's characteristics which we use as the basis for our traditional, practical approach is not based on reality. It is based on limiting assumptions. We reduce the complex reality by ignoring some of the basic facts of human nature. We have separated education from psychology and therefore do not know the child, even though much new information is available. Education is usually defined as the answer to the questions: "What do we do to and for the child?" It does not emphasize the question, "What does the child bring to this process?" "Who is this child?" "How does the child feel about the process?" Traditional education really concerns itself primarily with the extension of the child's personality, with the child's skills and ability, with what the child can do and not who the child is.

And yet, we are surprised when our children become reluctant followers, and wonder why we find so-called underachievers, so-called behavior problems, and school dropouts. Only if one of these failures occurs, do we move the focus slightly from the behavior to the child and try to identify something about the specific learner. Even then we are not really looking for the person, but only for a part of him, the academic learner. We administer standardized tests. We compare achievements of all the children of the nation, assuming they all function the same way. Therefore, we consider this particular child the exception. We do not look at each child as unique, but rather we call the child who differs "a problem."

However, at this point we may realize that the test results do not tell us what the problem is, why the difference exists. The tests do not give us the complete answer to this particular child. Thus, we may again move over our focus a little bit more and test the child's intelligence. Again, we are asking what can the child do, not who the child is. Therefore, a whole different set of tests is being used, and still, we find that we do not understand certain areas of reaction in this child. Next we realize that in this particular case there are parts of the personality which are different from the intellect, and again, we use other tests. We use a test to evaluate the creative ability of the child. After all these tests, have we defined the child? No, we have not. We have taken the academic person apart, and we have tried to develop each of these parts, but we have never put the child together again.

Not only do we never look at the whole, we do not even look at all the parts. We look at intellectual, creative and physical abilities. We look at what the child can do, but we still have not looked at who the child is. If none of these tests helps in the education of this particular child, we say that the answer belongs in the field of psychology, not education, and is therefore out of our jurisdiction. We look at the field of psychology as separate from education, and we therefore do not include the psychology of the child in the educational process. This means education does not know the child.

How can we educate without knowing who the person is? No business would develop a process without knowing what it is they are trying to develop and the characteristics of the material they are using. Yet this is exactly what education attempts to do. Parents and teachers, with the best of intentions, put the greatest emphasis on the child's ability to perform, on what he can do, forgetting that who the child is influences what the child can do. We rarely ask who this total person is, or who we think and feel he is, and even less, who the child thinks he is.

PROCESS OF EDUCATION:

Over the years, the process of education has been developed based on the previously described lack of philosophy and unrealistic concept of who is being educated. We have decided on certain subject matter as being important, beginning with the basics. We follow a definite sequence using predetermined programs, in which the child is expected to march lock-step from kindergarten through twelfth grade. These expectations are true for each and every child, without regard to his historical or personal background, his characteristics or present needs, or his personality. A huge superstructure of teaching programs has grown out of this: workbooks, text books, tests, learning programs, computers, etc. An enormous industry depends completely on all of these assumptions. This industry requires research in what to teach, not what to learn and how to learn. Industry as well as individual devoted teachers invest enormous amounts of time, money and energy in developing these materials.

We develop prescribed programs which begin in kindergarten and sometimes go all the way through high school, and feel that each child has to go through them exactly in the manner in which they are presented. In some way education, and with that the individual child, is now owned by the educational industry, by the education business. This seems unalterable, regardless of the needs of the individual child, or even of the school.

Such a rigid uniformity dictates that an American school which exists in some foreign country will follow the prescribed course so that the children can graduate from any American high school. An American child may grow up in an international school in Hong Kong and never learn anything about the Chinese culture. The same is true in other places. This is living proof of an education alienated from life. Expensive books and equipment, including computers and many other learning machines, will be shipped all the way across the world, while free living and learning opportunities immediately available in front of their eyes will be unseen or ignored. The opportunities to learn about different cultures or to expand horizons by learning about the immediate surroundings will not be used in these schools. Traditional education makes very few attempts to bridge education to life outside the classroom.

Any child or group who does not fit into this universal, predetermined system is considered a problem or a misfit. Gifted children who learn concepts more easily than skills or who are ahead in one area and not doing so well in another, who do not fit into the preconceived pattern, will not be accommodated according to their needs. Children who have difficulties fitting into the system for various emotional or academic reasons, such as having difficulties learning to read at an age that has been pronounced an appropriate age for all children to learn to read, become failures and learn to look at themselves as such. We try to force them into the system by tutoring, therapy, or punishment. We say to children, "You may not go out and play until you have finished your arithmetic." This results, then, in double failures. If they do not have the opportunity to play with their friends, they will be outcasts from their friends' point of view; and they still will not have learned what they are supposed to learn. Tutoring may or may not make the difference, but the time it consumes limits their opportunity to excel in other areas.

If children want to pursue some areas that are not considered strictly academic, their opportunities again are limited. If there's not much money available, then art and music classes may be curtailed, field trips may not be allowed, and their special interests in science may not be supported. At the same time, because sports have always been included in our idea of a well-rounded person, especially competitive sports, money for uniforms will become available before money for an outstanding art teacher, etc. Many of these limitations and pressures to be part of a rigid, preset system have a hidden curriculum of mixed messages and value judgements and become the problems and difficulties that gifted children experience during their growing years.

FAILURE OF EDUCATION:

As I said in the beginning, society is unhappy with the state of education. It is looking for reasons for the perceived failure. In this criticism, we seem to look at the way in which we use our accustomed methods, not the methods themselves; the way in which we try to reach our accustomed goals, not the goals themselves, and we even blame the children as well as the teachers or the administrators for the failure. The failure of modern education can be seen most glaringly in the lack of motivation by many children. Natural motivation disappears after the children have spent several years at school, because we do not relate to that which really motivates them. We try to solve this by creating artificial motivations. We do not recognize that an education process based on outdated information will continue to fall short no matter how many different types of bandages we apply.

It is my belief that teachers and children are not at fault for the dilemma of education. The fault is to be found in the system itself. A way must be found to examine and redefine the three components of education so that they can once again be the solid building blocks of a sound educational system. Many public and private educators are aware of the problem and are trying different approaches. However, they cannot do it alone.

Society as a whole must recognize that the basic problem with modern education is that its goals, its understanding of the value of each individual, and its processes are on shaky ground, for they are based on a number of unexamined assumptions and notions.

UNEXAMINED ASSUMPTIONS

A. An unexamined concept of modern life.
B. Unexamined hopes and expectations for the future of our children.
C. A theory of education separate from life and modern realities.
D. Assumptions of characteristics of children which have long been disproved by psychology.
E. A rigid process which is based on the fore-going assumptions and whose results have remained basically unexamined. The process itself becomes isolated from both the goals to be achieved and the personality of the child who is to achieve them.

SUMMARY:

The result is that the whole system generates a great deal of failure, and even the successes, those children who do achieve in terms of the present goals of education, often do not succeed in terms of life. Educators cannot help but be aware of the number of children who fail, often in predictable ways, and are unable to learn within the system — not because they are not capable, but because their manner of learning is not compatible with the way they are being taught. They fail in the eyes of the system, and, unfortunately, also in their own eyes. They lose motivation. When this is reflected by their behavior, **they** are labeled "problems," rather than the system that truly deserves the label. Our remedies are usually more of the same. We give achievement tests, and then rank the children according to these achievement tests. We look for the difficulty within the child. We ask, "Why did the child not do well within our system?" rather than, "Is our system appropriate?" We use artificial motivation, such as marks, awards, praises or punishment, or disapproval and disappointment. We do not ask what happened to the natural motivation for learning which we see in every infant.

These failures can be documented by the large number of school dropouts and school failures. They can also be seen in more subtle ways: children who are unhappy, children who never reach their full potential, children who never succeed with anything they want to do. There are people who cannot participate in society; there are people who have difficulties living with their families, taking care of their children, etc. There are people who suffer from depression and stress. Of course, the educational system cannot and should not accept responsibility for all these ills of humanity, but it should decide whether and to what extent it needs to and can address them. It should determine to what extent, if any, academic success is really related to success in life.

Beyond this, and vastly more important, we need to take a global view in making our decisions, to look at the state of the world. It is in a state of chaos. We do not know how to handle our conflicts, personally, nationally, and globally. We use archaic methods of confrontation rather than cooperation. We don't know how to handle anger and aggression personally, nationally and globally. We live in a world whose prisons are overflowing, where murders, assassinations and terrorism have become commonplace, where nuclear weapons buildup can bring us to the brink of global extermination at any moment. Again, we cannot, of course, blame education for this state of affairs, but education cannot remain oblivious to it and cannot continue to isolate itself from it. Just as we have always isolated education from psychology, we are also isolating it from politics, and therefore, feel that global awareness is outside the realm of education. Yet, again, we must ask ourselves whether education does not have a task in helping the world and our children by preparing our children for the world's reality.

It has often been said that politics are made in the cradle. We should think about whether there is truth in this statement, whether what happens in our political life does not grow out of the early experiences of childhood, at home and at school. Does education have a responsibility for raising a generation which can cope with the world and understand its complexity and bring about the necessary changes?

If we believe this, how should we define the goals and philosophy of education? What should we know about the psychology of the modern child, and what methods should we use to carry out the new philosophy based on the characteristics of the modern child?

The following chapters will examine a philosophy of education, the unique personalities of children and their development, and, growing out of these concepts, a fundamentally different process of education.

A PHILOSOPHY OF SELF-ACTUALIZATION AND INTERDEPENDENCE

A philosophy of education is only relevant if it exists within a philosophy of life. In developing a learning and living community at Roeper City and Country School, we developed the following as a philosophy of both learning and life. At the same time, this philosophy also addresses self-actualization and interdependence.

> We are concerned with the whole impact of life on the young person and the impact the person will make on society. We are concerned with the development of the "Self" and the interdependence of all "Selves."

This philosophy originates from a combination of an idealistic commitment to equal rights and a realistic view of the limitation of power by our mutual interdependence. It provides a unifying principle. It is based on the following realization: there is neither absolute power nor complete dependence or independence. The fact of interdependence, or human ecology, becomes more and more apparent in today's world. All parts of the globe depend on one another economically, culturally and emotionally. All this, if followed through logically, translates into the compelling need for cooperative action. Yet most of our skills and beliefs are based on confrontation and competition. Most people function as though there were a hierarchy of human rights and human life-structures. There is a top to be reached by the few, built on a hierarchy supported by the many.

A philosophy which tries to develop the skills of cooperation, and looks at this as the ultimate moral and realistic goal, may be the only true approach that might keep the world from destruction. Out of this philosophy grew some specific goals for all members of the school community.

GOALS:

1. To protect the equal rights of each member within a specific community. This includes everyone who is involved in the community. The janitors, bus drivers, secretaries — all the support personnel — are just as

valued in a given situation as teachers, administrators, parents, and children.

Example:
The discussion of the structure of the lunch program within such a philosophy would include administrators, janitors, teachers, food servers, students, parents, and the dietician. The dietician knows what is healthy to eat. Teachers and administrators know the schedule. The janitor knows that rice is hard to pick up with a vacuum cleaner from a carpeted floor. Children know what they like. Out of all this information, a valuable lunch program would result. In addition, each individual who participated in it would feel that s/he has had a part in the planning and would try to help make it work. The overall approach to problem solving is based on a concept of participatory democracy. Whether it means large administrative or governmental decisions or smaller organizational ones, the basic principle is the same; nothing happens outside of it.

2. To create opportunities to develop the skills, attitudes, techniques and emotional acceptance of the concepts of cooperation and interdependence. To create an awareness of the chain reactions resulting from all human actions.

Example:
A substitute teacher had a great deal of difficulty working with a class of seven-year-old children. She complained to the director and threatened to leave right away. A director in this case could have scolded the children and punished them; however, in our philosophy model, she seriously discussed the situation with them. During this discussion the children said they felt mistrusted and uncomfortable due to being handled in a way which they were not used to. It was also revealed that the substitute teacher did not know that they were allowed to go to the bathroom without having a pass. Her expectation to give them a pass before they could go made them feel distrusted and very angry.

In the course of the discussion, the director also pointed out different ways in which they could have handled the situation and that their regular teacher was attending a performance of her own child and would have to be called back if the substitute left. This then would be a chain reaction which would affect them, their own teacher and the teacher's own child. There was no more trouble for the rest of the day.

3. To provide learners with a learning environment which will help them toward these goals, including new subjects and approaches relevant to modern life and relevant to the individual learner.

   This should include a global approach to all subjects. It should include languages, current events, geography, and many other areas which are not necessarily part of the traditional learning environment. In social studies, for instance, the study of world hunger, the study of the environment, and many other areas which the modern child is exposed to would be an integral part of the curriculum.

4. To provide the kind of living and learning environment which will help learners grow into people whose impact on the world will not have to be distorted, dominated, restricted, or even counteracted by their unfulfilled emotional and personal needs.

   Example:
   A little five-year-old boy arrived at our school with a habit of screaming and temper tantrums which tended to disrupt the whole program. After a month or so, he remained quiet in his classroom; and there were no more temper tantrums and screaming. When he was asked what had brought about the change, the boy said, "I now have channels. I can talk about what bothers me."

   How do we develop such an atmosphere? Basically by building an organization which is based on trust and not on distrust, by organizing one's priorities with this in mind, and by allowing time and accessibility for children and adults to express their feelings.

5. To develop a vision that encompasses the whole, and not just a part of it.
   Within this concept the teacher tries to base her interaction with children on the overall picture including equally her own needs, those of the individual child, the class, the school and society.

   Example:
   A very creative child has a tendency to use up a lot of paper in her projects and to surround her place in the classroom with it. She obviously needs this. The teacher has an inner need for tidiness. The

school has a need for paper to be saved and not wasted. Society needs her to learn to be considerate. Parents want her to be successful and cooperative. All these needs are valid. They all create pressure on each other—the parents, the child, the teacher and the school, etc. The teacher must look at all these valid needs and create an approach which would consider all of them in a positive way. One way might be to tell the child the overall problem and see if she can find a way to solve it.

6. To develop an understanding of one's rights and obligations within the interdependent community.

   For instance, in an interdependent school community it would not be taken for granted that the principal has a reserved parking space near the office, while the teachers who often carry heavy materials have to walk a longer distance. In the hierarchical tradition, the concept is accepted by everyone that our human rights increase as we climb up the organizational ladder. In an interdependent community everybody has equal rights whether they are children, support personnel, administrators, teachers or parents.

7. To see the community as a circle of interdependence rather than as a hierarchy of dependency.

8. To see peers and other community members as cooperators rather than competitors.

   This includes trusting support of the expertise of others. This also means valuing our diversity without feeling that we are inferior if others have skills and abilities that we do not have.

   Example:
   A teacher and a little girl had difficulties getting along with each other. The teacher needed to function within a well organized environment. The child was very creative and her actions irritated the teacher. In another room there was a child who needed a great deal of clear cut organization, clear cut directions. The teacher had a spontaneous approach to teaching which confused that child. The teachers realized that their teaching styles and the children's learning styles did not coincide. After careful discussion with parents and children, an exchange took place and both children were able to grow in their own way, while the teachers could function in their own way.

9. To see one's self as a member of the community in four important ways: to have a stake, to have a voice, to have responsibility and to fulfill a specific task — to see participation in the community as a whole, indeed, as a part of this task.

There are many daily opportunities and examples which show how members of the nonhierarchical, self-actualizing community live within this concept and how their community differs from a hierarchical community. However, it differs for each adult and his or her particular role and changes in kind as the young child grows older.

Example:
Adults are clearly responsible for the physical safety of young children on a play- ground. As the children grow older, however, the children can learn to take responsibility for their own actions and safety and begin to feel responsible for others. The teacher withdraws into the background to the extent that the children are able to take over for themselves.

In this context recess does not continue to be the period when children express their hostile and competitive feelings, but becomes one when their cooperative skills are being developed. Cooperative games can contribute to the development of these skills. In that case the adult who has learned these skills becomes the protector and guide rather than the punitive authority figure.

10. To see one's self as a valuable and valued member of the community.

IMPLEMENTATION:

A philosophy is only as valid as its implementation. It may be reflected in the community through the following ways:

1. Creating a governmental and administrative structure which reflects the philosophy and allows interaction to take place which furthers self-growth and cooperation.

2. Creating opportunities for children to participate in their destinies to the extent they are developmentally able.

Example:
At our school we had weekly representative meetings with small groups of seven and eight-year-old children. We would eat lunch together and discuss any kind of problem that arose in their small communities and they made suggestions and proposals, discussed the reasons, etc. Some of their proposals were very helpful and often they could see that rules and projects for their group or even the whole school grew from them. One of them was the cooperative creation of an adventure playground.

3. Seeing children as valid members of the community and respecting their rights and responsibilities, perceptions and thoughts.

4. Allowing freedom of exploration for children within the framework of expectations.

    This framework of expectations might be in some aspects different for each individual child. All aspects of learning and growing as an individual developmental process are emphasized rather than instruction alone. Out of this concept grows a different approach to curriculum and testing and a reevaluation of necessary skills and knowledge. Any evaluation should include all areas of growth rather than only academic ones because that immediately gives academics priority, due to the fact that only academics are being measured. In most programs for elementary children, reading is given priority over all other learning experiences, discounting any other developmental progress.

    This framework means a program which allows learners to participate in their destinies. It means a program which looks at education as the opportunity to grow rather than the necessity to fit preconceived expectations. It also means a program which builds bridges between the individual and the world.

5. Creating a program rich in opportunities for all kinds of growth — academic, creative, physical, social, moral and opportunities for joy — a program which combines who we are with what we can do.

6. Using an approach which stresses a global point of view and emphasizes mutual responsibilities, thereby requiring that children be exposed to the practical aspects of interdependence whenever the opportunity arises.

7. Building into all subject matters an emphasis on complexities of life and the fact that every experience, every action, every perception has many causes and many effects - that in truth, life is not a linear progression but an all-encompassing development in all directions.

    Subject matter must stress complexities rather than simple sequences. All subject matter should emphasize that every event, every thought, every fact is like a rain drop falling on water creating ever widening circles. Most education is based on sequential progression rather than on global understanding.

8. Including in all subject matter confrontations with moral decisions which grow out of our increased technical knowledge and our commitment to humanism.

9. Emphasizing the future is theirs to create.

    There is a whole growing body of future studies pro- grams which show how we can make our own future and how we are responsible for it.

10. Emphasizing all areas of communication: openness, mutual understanding, verbal (language, literature, writing), non-verbal (dance, art, music), first-hand experience (travel, contact with people from different walks of life, off-campus jobs and instruction for older students, etc.), involvement in the events of the moment: political, social, cultural.

11. Looking at the school as the world in microcosm where all the conflicts, problems, solutions, inter- dependence and chain reactions exist in a similar way that one finds in the world at large as well as using these opportunities to create learning experiences for the children and to enhance the scope of the community by letting students make an impact through student government structures and other channels.

One might argue that living in such a community does not prepare one for the so-called real world which is in most part competitive and not cooperative. However, people who grow up in a cooperative world where they feel supported and respected develop a positive self-image and an understanding of who they are and their strengths and potential as well as weaknesses. They develop an understanding that even though they live in a competitive world they will not be defined by it. These people will be able to cope with it better, bringing with them more internal and external resources than anyone who has never had a chance to make an impact and whose self-image depends only on climbing the ladder of success.

This philosophy is not a vague and sentimental idea of warmth and understanding. It represents not just a desire for happiness and a good life, although in a much broader sense these hopes are part of it, but actually a relentlessly demanding concept, for its consequences are most complex, intellectually, emotionally and practically. One is always in danger of contradicting this philosophy or losing it altogether without realizing it, by making small compromises which have a tendency to grow and yet may only solve the problem apparent at the moment. Such compromises may exclude more difficult solutions within the philosophy which are not found because they are not looked for.

Built into this philosophy are both constancy and change. Its inherent goals remain constant while the implementation may change as times and life require. If constancy is not maintained or change does not occur, the result will be a philosophy which is mere lip service, irrelevant or non-existent.

THE REALITY OF THE SELF

Human beings have an enormous desire to be understood and recognized as legitimate members of their environment. They need to feel that their unique "Self" is acceptable, and to understand that they are entitled to this acceptance. Many struggle to be heard but seldom feel this to be the case. They carry with them a feeling of discomfort that arises from not being understood. Why are they not understood? This is caused, among other things, by the structures with which they are surrounded. The structures which surround the child for many years are the educational institutions.

DEFINITION:

In conventional educational literature one finds little, if any reference to the "Self" of the child, because the emphasis is on teaching rather than personal growth. There is not even a word for this inner unit as an existing concept within the educational community.

Literature, philosophies, religions, and psychiatry have been preoccupied with the "Self" or the "Soul" through the ages. Psychoanalysis and other branches of psychiatry, on the other hand, have tried to define the essence of human beings in many different ways. Religion uses the word "Soul." What, then, is this "Self?" I would say that in the last analysis it is a mystery. Neither we ourselves, nor those around us will ever understand it in its entirety, but the fact is that it exists, and it is a reality. There is something in each of us which reacts as a whole, something that is a unit in itself and follows its own course of development. It's what each of us considers the "I." It's what feels and thinks, experiences and reacts within us. It is the "I of the beholder." Everything that comes our way filters through it and becomes changed by it. Several people witnessing the same event will each come away with a different experience or different images and different memories. And yet, they shared the same outward experience. They each see it from their own point of view, through their own feeling of "I," of "Self." This is why we so often question, "What is reality?" for we each have our own. Yet each is an indisputable experienced reality, a reality of feeling, not necessarily a reality of fact. This often makes the reality of facts hard to determine. The reality of feelings is a fact in itself. It depends on the unique individual "Self" and its state and development of the moment.

DEVELOPMENT:

How does the "Self" develop? How does it grow? Much has been written about the "Self" in psychology, psychiatry, and psychoanalysis. It is not my intention to describe the whole literature on the subject and all the different points of view. I really only want to point out the existence of the unique "Self" and its central position in the growth of individuals and how they experience life. My own perception of the unique "Self" has grown from experience as well as from experts in the field and existing literature.

Where does the "Self" originate? I don't think anybody really knows how this feeling of the inner unit actually originates. I believe it possibly originates and grows in the womb along with the physical body. Its first experience in the outside world is its reception at birth. Children experience themselves as the parents perceive them. It is this perception which makes an impact on the structure of the "Self" and will allow the "Self" to grow or to remain small and underdeveloped. The way people feel about themselves depends on how others feel about them. Just as our standards, goals and conscience are a reflection of the standards, goals and attitudes of those around us and of society in general, so do we incorporate and accept the way in which we feel about ourselves from our significant surroundings. This, in turn, depends on how the parents feel about themselves, how their "Self" has been nurtured by their family. The "Self" has a hunger of its own, a need to be supported and recognized in order to grow. We speak about food for the body, food for thoughts. We also need to feed the "Self."

SELF-IMAGE:

Out of the "Self" develops the self-image. The self-image grows out of the basic unique feeling the person has about himself. Only if there is a "Self" can there be an image. Therefore we can say, the "Self-image" is a part of the "Self," but not the "Self" itself.

A person's "Self-image" consists of both the conscious and unconscious feelings and opinions about oneself. For example, a person could feel consciously that he or she is beautiful, bright and popular, and unconsciously that he or she is basically inferior, disappointing, without rights or power. It could also be the other way around. Consciously a person could feel inferior yet unconsciously feel really superior, but suppress it for fear of competition with someone, such as a sibling. Any acknowledgement of the person's "Self" makes an impact on the "Self-image." Growth and development of the "Self" is intertwined with and part of physical, intellectual, and emotional growth. The living/learning environment can allow this growth to happen, or can become a hindrance to it.

Example:

A woman was one of eight children, and always saw herself as the odd one, the ugly one, the angry one, a misfit in the family structure. But, on several occasions, her father gave her the impression that he understood how she really felt, and that he had a special relationship to her. All her life, she somehow lived by the thought of the secret link that existed between her and her father. It gave her the basis of a good "Self-image" of whom she was; but this basis was not enough to the "Self," for her father died early and she perceived her environment as unsupportive. For the rest of her life the secret link with her father sustained her, but not enough to counteract the perception of an uncaring environment.

ACTUALIZATION AND INTERDEPENDENCE:

The "Self" is entitled to its own development. If we ignore its existence in daily interaction we are stunting its development. The "Self" is not part of the official definition of the individual as viewed by most family, social, political, and educational institutions. Instead, individuals are usually defined by their known characteristics and abilities, by what they can do, not who they are. Therefore, the "Self" is like a caged bird that can't come out. Often the environment denies the existence of "Self" and creates disbelief that the uniqueness of the individual has a place in it.

The entitlement of the unique "Self" is true for everyone. This is contrary to the point of view which is based on a hierarchy of value of human beings. For instance, we speak of lower classes and upper classes and automatically connect different values to them, along with different values to the "Self" and its development. Extreme examples are the current system of apartheid in South Africa or the way the Nazis viewed the Jews.

A whole group of people is devalued by the creation of a hierarchy. Those on the bottom are assumed to be less worthy and are believed to have less feeling than others. In extreme cases their lives are considered to be less valuable than those with higher status in the hierarchy. Often those on the bottom accept this judgment themselves. They, therefore, develop a lesser "Self-image." Only if we recognize mutually the intrinsic equality of each "Self" will we allow all or any "Selves" to develop; for a real "Self" does not depend on the devaluation of others.

There is a mutuality built into the self-actualization approach based on the interdependence among people. The right of the development of the "Self" exists within the commitment of mutuality. The individual is never seen as independent of the world. He is seen as a member of the world community who gives others what is given to him—the right to a soul, a "Self."

This point of view diffuses the argument that "Self" development leads to selfishness. When a child grows up with empathy he develops empathy. Empathy is the connecting link from one human to another. This in turn leads us to a global point of view, a point of view that includes all human beings as having equal rights to "Self" development.

It is in this way that education for self-actualization actually leads to education for interdependence and cooperation.

The Development of Self:
Viewing the Child From the Inside Out

This chapter talks about the difference between looking at one another from the inside out or from the outside in and the impact this has on the development of the "Self." When we try to see each other from the inside out we allow the "Self" to develop. When we see each other from the outside in we deny this development.

At first the growth of the "Self" depends on the interaction between the parent and the "Self" of the child, and later, as the child matures and grows, from interactions between the "Self" of the child and other individuals. However, our task as parents and educators is often defined as caring for the child's physical needs and skill achievement; and we take the development of the emotions and the "Self" for granted. Child and parent have a number of tasks in their development of the relationship to each other's "Self" which changes as they both grow and change.

SEPARATION:

The first one, and the one on which all others depend, is the proper separation of the two "Selves", of mother and child. Birth means the moment of separation, both physically and emotionally. The miracle has occurred, as a new small separate physical person appears, i.e., the nucleus of an I, a small self, the nucleus of a "Self-image". No longer will the body be fed inside the mother. The baby may still be nurtured through the mother physically and emotionally, but as a separate human being. This initial emotional separation runs parallel to the physical separation. The child must be nurtured for himself in order to grow emotionally and physically.

This initial emotional separation is difficult for both parent and child, and takes place in different ways. Both parents often see their children as extensions of themselves and, therefore, are not separated. At times separation does not take place at all, and in that case, a symbiotic relationship remains for a long period, in which neither child nor parent can see the line between them, nor can they see themselves or the other as a separate entity. At other times the separation may take place very slowly, or it may take place late, or it may take place in parts only. It may not proceed evenly, with the development of other parts of the person, such as the development of specific skills, information, and other relationships. It is, in any case, a long, slow process, and a process which is never completely finished. The process progresses differently in relationship to the manner in which the original separation has taken place at birth. A parent's feeling of love is different if the parent loves the child as part of the parent's own self or as a separate autonomous human being.

The manner in which the individual "Self" reaches out to the world depends on the original basic parent-child relationship. The "Self" is motivated by its own need to develop. From the day of birth, the small "Self" begins to stretch and grow. The motivation to learn in young children is amazing to watch. No one has to push them into learning. Incentive and rewards are not necessary, for their reward is mastery over their own bodies and the world around them. Their "Self" is growing through this mastery.

The parents' task is to help the total child grow in all areas, and protect him until he can protect himself, so that he can become a member of the world by gaining his identity as an individual. If the parents' own emotional needs have been fulfilled, they can enjoy the miracle of growth of the new person, and this joy is transferred to the child. Even parents whose own needs have not been fulfilled are often able to separate and develop an independent love and respect for this human being who came from them. He is allowed to exist for himself. He is allowed to grow unencumbered. Every subsequent interaction will either add to this feeling of "Self" or take away from or change it.

The child grows, develops and learns physically, intellectually and emotionally against the background of the free or burdened "Self," which means the background of interaction between parents or other adults and the child. If the child is conceived of as an independent human being, the skills and achievements acquired with growth become part of and add to the "Self." If the "Self" feels he is part of the parent, and has to nourish the parents, then these skills and achievements are added to the parent's "Self." The child's individual "Self" will receive the skills and achievements only to the extent that he is a part of the parent.

The growing "Self" is exposed to the "Self" of the parent and also to realistic events beyond the parent's control, such as illness, wars, etc. It is also exposed to the particular social environment in which the child lives and to society in general. These circumstances may be in contradiction to the needs of the child. If the child's "Self" is being perceived by the parents as an independent unit, outside influences will be dealt with in a manner in which they will add to the child's growth and ultimately to the child's "Self." In other words, the basic tools of educating the child's "Self-imaging" are empathy and understanding of the child's feelings about himself. At first the child's "Self-image" is mirrored in his reception by the parents. Their love for him makes him love himself. Slowly, he separates and incorporates this love in himself.

If we nurture the child with love and empathy and protection, he will in turn learn empathy and return it to adults. In the language of psychology of the "Self," this interaction is called mirroring. If the mother's face is unclouded by her own need, the child sees only himself and her joy in his existence in her eyes. If her face is clouded, there will be no reflection or a distorted one, and that is the way in which the child will see his "Self." Quick separation would be harmful. No separation would also be harmful, because it would deprive the child's "Self" of a necessary learning experience. Careful, well-timed separation with empathy will lead to self growth.

INTERACTION:

As the healthy "Self" grows and develops, the child internalizes the love by others, and continues to learn to love himself, and feel well-nourished, content, and strong. This serves as a cocoon against assaults from the outside world. As the child interacts with his ever-widening world, experiences are not life-threatening, but in contrast, growth-producing, for his feeling of "Self." A normally developed "Self" does not mean that the child will have no conflicts, no emotional reactions, etc. Sometimes the emotional reactions will be stronger because they are allowed. It means being able to handle the emotions and experiences appropriately and not be overwhelmed by them.

According to Jean Piaget's theory, the ability of the young child to think is yet immature. In the first stages of his development, he cannot represent reality by retaining images. Therefore, the infant believes that when his mother leaves him, she is truly gone. He cannot conceive of her being in a different place. He reacts with terror. The task of the infant is to learn to understand that his mother exists even if she's not visible to him. This may be difficult for the mother to understand because she, of course, knows she exists and will return. The child does not know this. If the mother recognizes this terror and accepts it as real, the child will feel understood, and it will help him feel secure enough to somehow believe that maybe she will return. This means her empathy is a tool for learning. This empathy shows itself by physical contact, by a smile, by reassuring words. Even though he may not understand the words yet, he will understand their feelings, and his feeling will carry him through the period of separation. The following are some examples of how children will react differently to the same situation according to the status of their "Selves".

Example 1:

Three three-year-old children are beginning their entrance into nursery school. All of them cling to their mothers, at first, and refuse to let them go. One of the mothers stays until her child becomes acquainted with the teachers and the physical surroundings. She leaves something from her purse with him, and after a few days, he can leave her for a short while. He begins to relate to his teachers. Mother then leaves for a longer period, until the adjustment has taken place. The second child clings and cries and screams for weeks whenever his mother attempts to leave. She finally takes him out of school. The mother of the third child simply leaves. The child soon stops crying, sits in the corner, sucks his thumb, and accepts the situation as inevitable. He feels powerless to do anything about it.

Let's look at all of these cases in terms of the "Self." The first child probably has a well-developed "Self." He feels loved by mother, and loves himself. She showed empathy by giving him something that belonged to her, and by giving him time to adjust. He can face the newness and trusts mother to have chosen a safe environment for him. She considered his feelings, she allowed them to be developed in relation to the teachers; in fact, she somehow endowed the teachers with being able to be treated with trust just as she is. She transfers her own status with the child to the teacher. It was still difficult for him, but his "Self" was strong enough to deal with it. There are several explanations for the situation of the second child's "Self." He may not yet be strong enough to be away from home. The mother may have empathy with this and sense this and therefore not force the separation yet. Or the mother may need the child to heal her own wounds and "Self" needs. The child may be an extension of mother, and realizing this unconsciously, feels that his mother is not really able to separate from him. He may feel his role in life is to fulfill the mother's needs. He may not have developed an independent "Self"; in that case, all separations in the future will also be difficult. If it is simply a matter of development, and the mother's empathy tells her that realistically the child is not ready, he should be able to make an easy adjustment at a later time.

In the third case, the child does not feel the right to have his emotions. He does not feel that his mother supports him, and does not feel that he has any power. This child will have to find all sorts of substitute ways to fulfill his basic hunger, and there may be a great many difficulties in the future. In this case the child has a very deficient underdeveloped "Self." He feels his mother uses him for her own purposes, but does not care for him as a person. So he does not care for himself. Interestingly enough, this child may seem as though he is the best adjusted one, because he doesn't cry.

Crying, however, is really the healthy emotion. Even in the first case, it may be necessary, at a point, to leave the child crying. The mother may have to work, or the mother and teacher may decide that for the development of the child's "Self," the next step in the separation needs to take place, even though, and because, they have empathy with his feelings. He may be ready, but unable to take the step. At this point, the teacher shows the empathy, shows the understanding that separation is difficult, but necessary for growth. The child will be able to view the fact that his mother has to work as a necessary, possibly painful reality, but not as personal rejection. The teacher does not necessarily try to make him forget by getting him interested in other things, but shows her feelings for him and understands his. This empathy may lead to a variety of actions: the child may need affection or he may need respect for his pain by being left alone. Then, based on this acceptance on the teacher's part, the child may be able to move into the group and into other activities, or find his own manner to soothe himself.

Example 2:

Two children, three years old, each have a sudden attack of appendicitis, and have to be rushed to the hospital to undergo an operation. They are both gifted children, able to talk and able to understand the process to some extent. One child is anxious and upset over the procedure, and has a few nightmares following the operation. But he is interested in the process, he likes the explanations, and likes to understand how his body functions. He understands that the operation had to be done in order to help him. This child will have soon overcome his anxieties, for he has trust in his parents, and he realizes that the operation had to be done to cure him. His "Self" felt safe. His "Self" was not touched by this sudden experience. His cognitive ability supported this understanding, and made him able to master the traumatic experience.

The other child, also very bright, goes through a long period of sleeplessness, is unable to venture out, and feels enormously anxious and very guilty. This child did not see himself as protected or safe. He felt exposed to the newness in the hospital, the sudden operation, the pain, and felt that he had to deal with this all by himself, without knowing what it was all about. His "Self" felt powerless and unprotected. His giftedness only served to make him more threatened, because he was aware of what was happening to him and did not feel enough basic support. He also felt that it was his fault that he had to undergo this operation. It became proof of his notion that something wasn't right with him, that he was guilty of something, and it became a kind of punishment. After the operation, he became very subdued and quiet and kept proving that he was a good boy, because for him to be a good boy became a matter of survival. He feared being abandoned if he was not a good boy.

The other child, in contrast, may have gone through a rather active period, he may have become a little bit more aggressive, he may have been somewhat angry at his parents for not being able to protect him against having to have an operation, or for having to leave him in the hospital. He will be able to discuss the experience and express these feelings; and, in the end, the experience will become an addition to his "Self" growth, because he will realize he was able to cope with it well.

There are many stages in between these two types of "Selves" I have described. I think there are some you might call "in between Selves" and many of us might fall into that category. They will all of a sudden find that their image of themselves depends on the degree of their success and popularity but then again find their real security in their sense of "Self." I want to stress, however, that each unique "Self" is connected in many ways with the surrounding community and we do need the support and empathy of those around us. A well developed unique "Self" knows how to accept the support from the environment and use it to support the "Self." The reaction of parents and teachers will be interpreted by the child according to the status of his "Self."

Example 3:

Children are often reprimanded for not following a rule. One child interprets it as a repeated pattern of rejection. This may lead to self-rejection. This child feels that he is not good, and that he is not entitled to empathy and understanding. This child has a small, undeveloped "Self." Another child accepts the disapproval as realistic and may simply learn not to repeat the behavior. She does not experience it as a deprivation to her "Self," for her "Self" is not deprived. A third child may feel that the criticism was unjust, that in fact, he had not done what he was being criticized for, or that it was not his fault. In that case, he will express his outrage for the injustice, and speak openly about his feeling of being treated unfairly. This child also has a well-developed "Self." A child with an underdeveloped "Self" may feel it is unfair, but his "Self" is too insecure to react. He may also interpret the reprimand as unfair, but see the unfairness as his fault. He feels there is something which keeps him from having the right to be treated fairly.

A child is free to deal with growing and learning if he does not have to be concerned with the survival of the "Self." To make the "Self" feel safe is originally the task of the adults in his world, which they slowly turn over to him as he begins to internalize his parents' acceptance of him. It then becomes "Self" acceptance. The process is never entirely completed. The "Self" requires nurturing by others all through life, but if it has grown strong, it will not be a matter of survival.

On the other hand, a small undeveloped "Self" which has been allowed to go hungry can affect the whole growth and development of the person and the future life of the person's "Self." At times, this can affect a whole culture, or a number of people within the culture. Among the Jews during the Holocaust, the majority saw the German actions as a German problem imposed on them; but there were also those who felt that they truly had no rights and somehow accepted the German behavior as being caused by themselves. All through history, there are examples of acceptance of imposed inferiority by the people themselves, and by a person's "Self." This is frequently called identification with the oppressor. These people accept their imposed inferiority as real.

People who have an underdeveloped "Self" will believe that might makes right, and that those in power have a right to suppress the powerless, for they feel that powerlessness is caused by those without power. The lack of power in their minds is tied to the individual or groups and not the situation. These are the people who have a tendency to borrow their glory from someone else. They shine in someone else's light because they have no light of their own. Women in their traditional role borrowed their light from their husbands. For example, in Germany, a woman carried the title of her husband, as part of her own title. She would be addressed as Frau doctor, wife of the doctor, and her glory was achieved through her husband's title. People whose "Self" has been allowed to develop do not as adults need to spend time finding themselves. One might say they never lost themselves. But they might feel free to take the time to find their appropriate place in life. People with a strong "Self" will not be defined by money, power, or fame. They may value it, they may enjoy it, and they may use it; but their basic definition is their own well developed "Self." Those whose "Self" has not been developed may spend a lifetime unsatisfied, looking for the support, the verification they never received as they grew up.

THE SELF-ACTUALIZATION, INTERDEPENDENCE MODEL

AN APPLIED PHILOSOPHY:

Our philosophy took form in a new set of principles for operating a school. I shall call this set of principles the Self-Actualization, Interdependence Model (SAI model) for the remainder of the book. The purpose of the SAI model is to implement a structure which fulfills the following goals:

1. to help the child move toward self-actualization as opposed to preparation for college only,

2. to create an environment which allows this to happen through a cooperative way of life based on the fact of human interdependence.

These two goals are in themselves interdependent. A self-actualizing person grows in an interdependent community, and the interdependent community can only function well if its members are becoming more and more self-actualized and, therefore, able to truly function in such an environment.

Every atom is a replica of the physical world and vice versa. Every educational institution and even every classroom within it is structured like society in miniature. Within this structure develop the same basic forces of interaction as in society at large. Interaction and relationships within institutions of society, even though they exist often in democratic countries, are based on a power structure and hierarchy. Competition and cooperation function within and in relation to the hierarchical structure of each institution or government.

Within the hierarchical educational structures the goal is winning the competition whether the competition is getting the best marks or getting into the best college. Winning is the major goal and is most easily achieved by being more powerful or having better defenses and weapons. The ethics of how a goal is achieved or of the goal's greater, more long-term impact are of little or no concern in such a model.

Every child has a desire to win. We interpret this desire as simply being a part of growing up. This is only true in part. The desire to win is also a response of the child to the expectations of the environment. Children learn from our current environment that we live in a world where dog eats dog and might makes right. They learn how to cope with authority by accepting it or by rebelling against it; they learn to live with a concept of hierarchy and to aspire to reach its top. Even if an individual teacher functions within a different belief system, even if her classroom reflects her beliefs, it still exists within the hierarchical model, and the children are aware of it. Children develop the skills and emotional reactions to live in the hierarchical model and retain these skills throughout their lives. These skills and emotions do not in themselves constitute growth toward adulthood, but rather adaptation to a structure of hierarchy. The result is that children learn how to become cogs in the wheel of the power structure rather than becoming self-actualized adults living in an interdependent community. The structure in which a person lives contributes to the development of his or her personality.

In the hierarchical educational model, the child is at the bottom of the ladder. The teacher looks up to the principal, the principal to the superintendent. Decisions are often made in terms of pressures from above, rather than needs of the child. In this structure the child learns to please the teacher rather than to fulfill his own needs for "Self"-growth. He is motivated by trying to please rather than by his own motivations to learn and master. He learns about dependency and independence, not interdependence. The following is a remark from a gifted eight-year-old: "I cannot wait for vacation, because then I will have a chance to really learn."

For all of these reasons, we need to create a model which teaches the child skills of interdependence, a model which represents a different world in miniature, a future world, rather than reflecting the existing one and supporting the status quo. If we want the child to learn the skills of living and the skills of understanding global interdependence, he needs to live in an environment where they exist and where the adult possesses the same skills. If we want the child to grow up to consider all human rights as equal, he needs to live in a structure which exercises those rights. If we want the child to learn the skills of empathy and respect, he needs to live in an environment in which he is treated with empathy and respect. If we want the child to value his unique "Self," he needs to live in an environment where his "Self" is valued. Such an environment can only exist if the adults themselves feel uniquely valued and if they are validated by the structure. If we want the child to learn to make decisions based on justice rather than power, he needs to grow up in an environment where he can participate rather than powerlessly accept the decisions made by those in charge. One of the most frequent reactions of gifted children to traditional education is a pervading feeling of powerlessness. If we want the child to retain his innate motivation for inner mastery, he needs to live in an environment where this goal is recognized and supported, rather than one that imposes the goal of outside success.

It is obvious that we need to create a model with a basically different learning environment. In order to create this, we need a different definition of the overall governmental and administrative structure, a different definition of the tasks of the adult, a different definition of the curriculum, different methods of teaching and learning, and different goals for everyone involved. We need to be aware of this difference.

THE ROLE OF THE TEACHER IN THE SELF-ACTUALIZATION INTERDEPENDENCE MODEL

Within the framework of the self-actualization interdependence model, the adult role differs basically from the traditional one. The "Self" of this person becomes the central factor. Incorporated in this is expertise as a teacher, knowledge of subject matter, skill and technique in teaching, and personal excitement about children and learning. The personality of the teacher should be a factor not only in determining whether or not she should be teaching, but also in selecting the children to be in her charge. Certain teachers and certain children and certain parents are better able to work together than others, because both their personal needs and their personal characteristics complement each other.

By the time a child enters school, even nursery school, his "Self" has developed to some extent. He receives the experience of school through the channel of his previous experiences. At this point a child may have already experienced some emotional deficit—certain needs are likely not to have been fulfilled. The needs remain in existence as an ever-present craving for fulfillment at every opportunity. Such needs are present in the child, the parent, and in the teacher.

From the parents' point of view, having children renews the hopes for the fulfillment of their needs. They have great expectations for themselves from their children. The same is true for teachers who are also parents. This is the explanation for the often-observed phenomenon that some educators may relate beautifully to other people's children, while they may have difficulty with their own. The specific needs of their own children might conflict with their own personal ones. The craving for basic acceptance transfers itself from one generation to the next. However, all of us may have varying needs, some of which are filled by parents, some by teachers and other adults.

Example:

A mother may have great understanding and empathy for her child, but having to change his diaper sickens her, just as her own mother resented changing her diapers. She cannot feel empathy when he cries because of the discomfort of being wet or soiled. She may postpone doing the task. He reacts to her feelings and accepts it as his own, and in the future anything dirty bothers him beyond a normal reaction. He does not like it because his mother did not like it. In every other respect she is delighted with her child and understands his emotions.

This child now arrives at nursery school and transfers many of his feelings from mother to teacher. However, he senses a difference in the reaction of the teacher from the reaction of his mother. After a few weeks, he develops a habit of getting his hands dirty, spilling things upon himself, etc., and all the time looking at the teacher, wondering how she will react. The teacher brings her own self to the situation. Her emphasis may be in the area of having to prove that she is a capable teacher. The child learns well and the teacher is not concerned with his messiness and is able to accept it. It is not her area of concern, and unwittingly she may help him to accept himself better. He experiences that he is no longer in danger of losing her support and after awhile messiness may not be a problem for him anymore. Teacher and child are able to fulfill each other's needs.

Many relationships between people, men and women, children and adults, are based on their ability to fulfill each other's deficits. If one person outgrows the need for dependency and the other person in a relationship still needs to be depended upon, conflicts arise. The same is true of a relationship between teacher and children.

The basic structure of the educational institution in most cases is based on learning the prescribed curriculum. Each member of the hierarchy in a traditional institution, such as teacher, principal, and superintendent, depends on the success of the curriculum with the child. In other words, the child is expected to fulfill the need of all of these people and of the institution to succeed. They all rest on the successful performance of the child. Empathy with the needs of the child or the teacher is not part of the concept. Into this structure enter the child and the teacher, each with their own needs and abilities. The problem for the child is that the teacher, whose need is often to prove herself to those above her in the hierarchy, has the institution on her side. The child's success becomes her success. Her success in teaching the child becomes the institution's success. The child has to fulfill these needs. Yet, in spite of this situation which can put a heavy burden on the child, it is remarkable how many children feel safe and supported by the teacher.

There may be two reasons for this. First, the teacher and the child fulfill each other's needs as described above. Second, a teacher with a very well-developed "Self," whose needs have been fulfilled to a large extent, is free to use her own creativity and empathy in terms of the child rather than for herself. She will be able to fulfill some of the unfulfilled needs of the child. This is often a second chance for children whose "Self" has been only partially developed, as in the example of the child whose mother was disgusted with having to diaper her child.

There is a great variety of ways in which children react to teachers. Some teachers are beloved by most children. If children are asked why they like a particular teacher, the answer most often is, "She likes me, she understands me." In other words, the child feels safe and supported. The second answer often heard is, "She is an interesting teacher and she helps me understand. She helps me learn through her knowledge." The teacher who knows how the children learn allows the children to own their knowledge. They learn for themselves and their success and growth reflects on the teacher, but the teacher is not defined by it. If the teacher is personally excited about the subject matter and wants to share it, both teacher and child can share the excitement about mastery.

In other instances, the needs of the teacher and the child conflict with each other. Such a mismatched situation often produces a child who seems disturbed. This child's problems become exaggerated because emotionally teacher and child are interfering with each other's needs. This child is desperate in his need and becomes more and more disturbed because the teacher cannot respond correctly, because of her own inner needs. However, if the child is moved into another room, with a teacher who happens to feel secure in this particular respect, often the problems become minimized, or disappear. Even if they don't really disappear, they may be handled appropriately by this particular teacher. This is often a reason why people can function well in certain situations and not in others.

All this is more so with a gifted child. These children feel more easily rejected; they are more easily misunderstood. They become more easily a threat to the teacher. Teachers feel that the gifted look through them and know when they are being manipulated and sometimes seem to sense things about the teacher which the teacher herself does not want to know.

The teacher also must recognize each individual child's "Self." She needs to understand the developmental stages through which the child is moving, and the child's unique approaches and abilities. Most gifted adults who see themselves as self-actualized say that one person in their life was most responsible in helping them grow freely. This could be a parent, a grandparent, a teacher, a school bus driver, a babysitter or a friend. That person often was not an expert in the area in which the child became accomplished, but one might say he was an expert in empathy with that child. The child felt supported and recognized by this person.

The most promising situation is when not only the teacher, but the entire school, the overall learning environment, reflects the respect and empathy for each individual self of any of its members: students, teachers, administrators, support personnel.

In this case, the central part of the curriculum becomes the development and growth of all "Selves." Academic skills, communication skills, physical skills and creative expression in this model serve the growth of the "Self" by working toward self-actualization of the child and the community. The goal is to allow the "Self" to grow with a minimum of deficits, to develop the self-potential to the highest degree possible. The intellectual, physical or creative potential become part of the growth of "Self." The rich learning environment, the resources, the teacher expertise and subject matter knowledge all can become channeled toward unified growth. A "Self" which has been allowed to grow in such an environment can deal adequately and appropriately with experiences that confront it; it is the prerequisite for reaching the potential in other areas. Often only when we reach our self-potential can we reach our creative and intellectual potential.

THE ROLE OF THE TEACHER IN RELATION TO THE GROUP

A teacher deals not only with the individual child, but with groups of children and group activities. Groups develop a "Self" of their own, a certain unique atmosphere and personality, which differs from group to group. The atmosphere grows out of the interaction between all of the members, including the teacher, but it is more than the sum of the interaction of all its members. It is interesting to observe how a group changes with the addition of a new member or the absence of another. It also changes with the absence of a teacher or the presence of a new teacher or a substitute teacher.

A group within the SAI model differs in nature from the traditional success dependency model. It is through the group that group members learn about the process in which the community functions. In the traditional model, children sit at assigned desks and little interaction takes place in the classroom. The group relations usually develop at recess with the teacher only participating to keep children from physical harm and to stop fights from erupting. A structure soon begins to develop within the group and a pecking order is usually established. Often a leader appears with his following. Sometimes groups of boys become gangs and terrorize others, especially the girls. Everyone soon acquires a role. There are the leaders, the cliques, the in groups, the outsiders, the followers, the manipulators, the show-offs. Even the peace maker and the carrier of grudges are some of the self-assigned roles. The basis of such a group is usually the power principle.

Children learn from their surroundings and function on the principle of hierarchy. The strongest or most clever becomes the leader. Standards of behavior are set by the group leader. At times this structure allows and brings out asocial behavior in order to impress the leader or because aggressive impulses have been suppressed and may come to the surface under such leadership. On the other hand, if the leaders are socially responsible, they may influence the group in that direction. Everyone may be supportive of the needs of the weaker ones because the leadership wants it that way. In that case the sense of responsibility rests on the outside rather than inside the individual.

I remember visiting a nursery school once where I saw a group of rather large four-year-old boys monopolizing the slide. Several little girls came over and obviously wanted to use it, but, after they took one look at the situation, they quietly left the scene without even trying to use the slide. It was obvious that they had experienced this before and had accepted the superior strength of these boys as the natural reason for monopolizing the slide. A few minutes later a teacher saw what was happening and told the boys to leave and give the girls the slide. The whole interaction was based on power. First the power of the big boys and later on the power of the teacher. In the SAI model, the teacher would call the children together, present the problem and allow them to express their thoughts and feelings. This would have empowered the girls to stick to their rights and help the boys to understand their own motivation as well as their responsibility and the consequences of their actions. The teacher would become the protector and the facilitator. This solution is only available if the overall atmosphere reflects community standards of cooperation.

Groups within the SAI model are based on cooperation. The skills of cooperation are learned by experience just like the skills of living within a hierarchy. In our school, children were given the opportunity to learn these skills inside and outside the classroom. Children had the opportunity to interact socially within the classroom because it was organized differently from the traditional classroom. The teacher observed and helped them with their social interactions on the spot, not by making authoritarian decisions, but by taking time to discuss the situation with them, to point out how the other person might feel, to give them opportunities to become acquainted with each other's reactions and feelings. In this model, leaders also develop, so do peacemakers, so do troublemakers, etc. But they all function within a certain philosophy and they are consciously exposed to the impact of their activities on others. They learn to understand how their actions, in the end, come back to them in a different form.

Relationships require empathy and need to be considered part of the learning process. Group discussions are one of the important means of achieving this. This also includes learning to interpret body language and other signals of distress or joy. The goal is for children to learn to feel both empowered and responsible within the groups and to see themselves as equal interdependent members. They need to see their own needs, take responsibility for their own actions and those of others. In that type of situation leadership grows out of expertise and may change from one to the other depending on the experience of the moment. This type of leadership is voluntarily accepted by the group. The teacher is often the leader and guide who is seen as an expert in most ways and as the adult who is their protector and support. In that situation the group and teacher work together rather than developing an antagonistic attitude which is so often the case. The teacher is also an authority, but her authority is based on the acceptance that exists between a group and the teacher and on the knowledge that opportunities for learning and growth can only be afforded by the teacher. In other words, the relationship must be based on mutual respect and trust.

Both George Roeper and I conducted so called "human relations" classes with the children. These would take different forms depending on the situation. We would either tell a story with a human relations problem to be solved by the group, or a member of the group would bring up some concern of his or her own, or a concern of the whole group would be discussed. The group members learned to express their thoughts and feelings and to help each other to find solutions. It was amazing how often their eyes would be opened to the needs or particular feelings of another child and how their ability to empathize developed. Under most circumstances, in different types of group settings children are not used to discussing such matters. Through this process, the youthful concept of seeing others as either good or bad, enemy or friend, gave way to a more complex understanding of the personalities, needs and problems of other human beings — including the teachers.

Children develop an understanding of the concept of interdependence of all human beings. They develop an understanding of the fact that no one is perfect and that we can help each other to deal with these imperfections, rather than be critical of them. This helps them accept their own imperfections which is especially important for gifted children who have a tendency to feel that they are obliged to be perfect. They also find out that others have sympathy for their imperfections and that showing themselves as they really are often increases friendly relationships and support. It affords them the opportunity to express negative feelings without hurting others, to accept them as real and permissible in themselves, to find ways to cope with them. They find out that expressing feelings in words often relieves them and makes it unnecessary to keep the feelings inside, where they can fester and grow. They learn that by discussing problems and facing them, they can often solve them and then forget them.

Example:

Sophy, a heavy-set girl, became known as the classroom bully. The other children were afraid of her. At times she would push the other children out of her way in order to get through the door first. The other children were so afraid that they accepted it. Even the teachers felt somewhat threatened by this child. This supported Sophy in acting and feeling unrealistically powerful and created more temptation for her to bully other children.

On one occasion, one of the children in the group asked me to help them resolve the problem of Sophy. Several other children suggested that the group should talk about that situation. I asked Sophy how she felt about an open discussion. She said that she would really like to discuss the problem and that she would like to be present. The children's desire for open discussion showed that they believed in the process.

In the session, the children began to complain about Sophy bullying them and stated that they were all afraid of her. I became somewhat concerned at this point, wondering whether I could keep this discussion from becoming a kangaroo court and not sure whether I should have allowed this situation to happen. My fear was unfounded.

Sophy began to cry and said, "How would you feel if everybody called you 'Fatso?' How would you feel if other girls looked so much prettier than you do? How would you feel if clothes that looked nice on others didn't look nice on you?" A whole new person evolved in front of all of us. It was amazing to see how the children could suddenly see this child, whom they had always considered mean and dangerous, as a suffering, insecure human being. They immediately answered with such expressions as, "You may be big, but your face is pretty." or "You are one of the best actresses in the school." They began to realize that her reactions toward them were motivated by fear, anxiety and anger, and that her bigness was the only way in which she felt superior to them, even though it also made her feel inferior.

Sophy's openness prompted other children to speak about their own feelings, their fear of her, their anger at her, and also about their own insecurities such as feeling that they were not pretty, that they were not as good a dancer as others, etc. That session ended with a true understanding among all of them and with a resolution—at least for the time being—on Sophy's part to stop bullying and on the part of the other children to interact with her in a friendly manner. Such things do not last forever and it was necessary to talk about the same problem on subsequent occasions. Through such processes children learn to see each other from the inside out.

Another Example:
A group of eight-year-old children came to me to discuss a problem. They said, " John is a nice boy, but he talks so much. He never gives anyone else a chance. He interrupts us all the time. What do you think we can do about this?" At this moment we happened to hear someone talking out in the hall. One of the

children said, "There he is, talking again as usual." Immediately another of them said, "Let's ask John to come in and tell him our problem."

One of the children went out to get him and, in a very friendly manner, said, "John, we are here to talk about you. We have a concern about you. You know that we all like you, don't you?" And this was true. John said, "Yes, and I like you, too." And he went on talking and talking, telling them why he liked them. I waited for the children to react. Someone said, "John, you're doing it again. That is the reason why we're here." He stopped, blushed and said, "Oh, now I know why you're here. You think I talk too much. I know that. I can't help it. I try not to. My mouth just runs away from me. Sometimes I don't even know it. Can you help me?" And the children said, "Would you like us to help?" He said, "Yes, I really would."

One of the boys suggested the following: "Why don't we agree that every time you forget and talk too much, one of us, or even more than one, will lift his finger and wink with it. And that will be a signal for you that it is time to stop." John said, "I would like that very much."

Everyone was pleased with that solution. As in Sophy's case, the solution did not last for more than a few weeks, but the important thing was that there was a problem awareness on the part of all of the children involved, and that it was accepted as a problem one could deal with. John had learned that criticism did not relate to his inner "Self," but only to a habit that was annoying others. The other children had learned a technique of criticizing one another which created channels of communication rather than wells of hostility.

These children learned techniques of careful social interaction, techniques which did not lead to antagonism, but to cooperation based on mutual respect. The children were pleased with what they had done. They felt that they had power, that they were listened to, they saw that they could make a difference. One child learned to accept criticism. These skills can be learned in many situations within a school community.

CURRICULUM IN THE SELF-ACTUALIZATION, INTERDEPENDENCE MODEL

This chapter describes the SAI approach to curriculum content and how it differs fundamentally from the traditional approach. There are many variations in between the two approaches. However, these variations are usually seen as elaboration or enrichment of the traditional model, not as representing a different principle. The SAI model is structured according to a different principle: education for life. As a result, the SAI curriculum differs in four fundamental ways from the traditional curriculum: the goals, the definition of learning, the content, and the methods.

THE GOAL:

The goal of the SAI model has been discussed earlier at some length. Therefore, it will suffice at this point just to mention the basic difference. The traditional goal of education is education for college and career. The goal of the SAI model is education for life. This means to provide the learner with opportunities for total personality growth within the conceptual framework of all aspects of global interdependence. This does not exclude preparation for college and career, but puts it into a different context and perspective.

THE DEFINITION OF LEARNING:

The traditional definition of learning is intellectual acquisition of material through information to be gathered, problems to be solved, skills to be mastered. This approach is cognitive only. The definition of learning in the SAI model is integration of material. Integration takes place through all senses. It is a combination of intellectual, emotional and physical mastery, which includes and goes beyond cognitive mastery.

THE CONTENT:

The traditional curriculum centers around skills. The SAI curriculum centers around conceptual frameworks. These frameworks are designed to provide the learner with an overall organization which facilitates the development of the learner's ability to understand and cope with his increasingly complex world. For instance, the function of a room in a house can only be understood in relation to other rooms and within the concept of house and family. Learning only about a bedroom does not provide an overview. Learning about the part in isolation is not as meaningful as learning about it in reference to the whole. The task of the school, therefore, is to create conceptual frameworks around all learning experiences which accommodate all learning styles and skills.

Some children, especially the gifted, are conceptual learners. They will often understand the concept and know little about the details. Others are learners of details and know little about the overall concept involved. Some children can define why cats are animals, while others will know the detailed habits of cats. The SAI model adds the principle of the conceptual framework to the learning process for all methods of learning.

RATIONALE:

The rationale for the concept-centered approach is both psychological and philosophical. All children look for a conceptual framework upon which to build their image of life. If we observe young children as they grow, we will see that they are struggling to make sense of this world. They look for a structure that will provide some type of order, for only then can they begin to master this unknown chaos cognitively and emotionally.

Gifted children are global thinkers and have a tendency to understand an overall concept at an early age. Others may not grasp a concept cognitively, but intuitively make it their own. The word "love" is an abstract concept which a young child cannot yet define, but the child feels good when someone says, "I love you." The framework "something that makes you feel good" is enough for now. The more detailed, complex definition can be added later. Young children also use the word "hate" appropriately with meaning as a word to hang their feelings on, even though they cannot truly define it. These become familiar, comfortable words which have meaning and create frameworks.

Actually, the need for a framework is so great that children begin developing their own long before they enter school. Thus they may have some unsound frameworks which are really misconceptions. The influence of misconceptions and the attitudes they foster are often difficult to change. The SAI model helps to restructure such frameworks along with guiding the building of other frameworks to avoid future misconceptions.

EDUCATIONAL PROCESS:

The SAI model's approach helps the child make the outside world part of his inner world. It is designed to help the child gain enough understanding, knowledge and confidence to integrate and master the outside world and make it his own. It is also designed to provide opportunities for the child to make an impact on the outside world and to feel accepted by it. The essence of this approach is the combination of the individual's growth and development of membership in the world community with all the rights and obligations this entails.

CONCEPTUAL FRAMEWORKS:

The following concepts are not seen or taught as part of a specific subject in the SAI model, but are integrated into many activities and living and learning experiences. They are used to create an overall conceptual framework. The learning takes place in many different ways on different occasions through a variety of methods. They are, however, described under certain traditional subject matter headings in order to create familiar guidelines for the reader.

The descriptions below are not designed to serve as a curriculum, but only as examples of concept learning. The descriptions are written in terms of material for young children in preschool and early elementary school, because the concepts involved form the foundation on which later learning and concepts are based. Other concepts are added at a later time, some expanding on earlier ones. It should be emphasized that even though this material is tailored for young children, the approach is valid for older children as well and can be used as a model for further development. Concept learning continues throughout life. Appropriate ages are not assigned to the concepts presented here for it depends on the developmental phase the children are in as well as the overall learning environment in which they grow up.

There are other basic concepts more relevant to certain groups of children or to certain cultures. The ones presented here have been developed through my observation and work with young children as well as the work of others.

I am not giving lists of resources, because I believe that teaching as well as learning is a creative act. Teachers need to have a framework of what needs to be achieved and to trust themselves to teach within it. Teachers who develop their own approach, find their own resources, and draw from their own inclinations as well as those of children are more effective teachers and enjoy teaching more, even though it may be more work.

Concept of Home and Family:

The first and fundamental concept the child experiences before entering school is family and dwelling. This is where the child belongs. This is the conceptual experience upon which the child bases safety and security. The child becomes familiar with the home environment during the first years of life. The child understands the physical properties of his dwelling and the habits and interactions of the members of the family. However, the concept of family is not yet well defined for the young child. Thus, he comes to his own conclusions. In addition, sometimes families teach children unrealistic concepts.

Example:

The family dog died and was replaced by a new one to ease the pain of the little girl whose pet it had been. The four-year-old girl became more unhappy rather than enjoying her new pet. It turned out that she saw the dog as a member of the family, like a brother or sister and felt disturbed over the fact one could simply replace a family member. It made her feel that she also could be easily replaced. When she understood that the dog was not truly a member of the family, because people families have people children and dog families have dog children, she also understood that, much as the family loved the dog, they did not love it in the same way they love her. She could now feel sadness for her loss without feeling concerned for herself.

Whether or not a young child can understand these concepts is often questioned. According to Piaget, the child may not yet be capable of multiple classification. And yet the child needs to understand that the dog can be part of her family, which is what she may have heard from her parents, and still belong to the dog's family. The explanation is that the dog belongs to the dog family, but dogs often live with human families. They are loved like a friend, but it is a different kind of love. Human children are born by their mothers who can only bear human children, not dogs. The child is classified as belonging to one family, the dog to another. Even if the child does not understand multiple classification, she can understand this, because the dog and the child are each classified only once.

The concepts suggested in this book can all be handled in a manner appropriate to children's developmental stages. The family unit becomes a prototype for all future learning. The child soon reaches out beyond the family and looks for broader units around his experiences to give them form and structure.

Concept of Animate and Inanimate Objects:

In order to accurately conceptualize and understand the structure of our world it is necessary to know the difference between animate and inanimate objects. Young children often struggle with whether objects are truly animate or inanimate. Opportunities to learn what constitutes the difference between these two states add to their ability to comprehend their global environment.

Concept of School:

School is another early, obvious concept. It is physically well-defined. A specified, well-known group of people occupy it for specific purposes. Children often come to school with misconceptions and very little understanding of what school actually is. Even as they get older, it is rarely specifically defined for them. They puzzle about why they go to school. Gifted children often ask the questions: "Do you go to get good marks? Do you go to school to learn how to read? Do you go to school to learn how to make money? What happens at school? Why is school run the way it is?" School is a concept that should be discussed frequently in different ways at different developmental levels.

Concept of the Earth:

Schools often begin their social studies projects with learning about the child's immediate environment. This is based on the existing belief that one should present children with material which is part of their experience. The usual sequence of study is city, state, country, Earth. However, the concept of city or the concept of state is not in itself a part of a child's experience. These concepts exist only in relation to others. The concept of state is based on the fact that it is a part of a country. The concept of country exists only in relation to the concept of Earth.

The SAI model begins with the concept of Earth with its natural boundaries. A country can then be understood as part of the Earth. Modern young children are confronted with information concerning the whole Earth early in their lives without having an understanding of it.

Concept of Geography:

Learning about the Earth fills two goals, the need of the learner for a surrounding framework and our goal for creating a basis for the awareness of global interdependence. The Earth is the framework within which our global interdependence takes place. The concept of the Earth as the home we all share gives children a framework within which to develop a meaningful structure for everything to which they are exposed. It is the concept which contains all of our lives and activities; this concept provides children with the opportunity to become more and more familiar with all the Earth's aspects and to feel at home and comfortable in an environment away from their own homes.

Learning about the Earth leads naturally into geography. Children are fascinated by globes and maps. There is a natural place for them in all classrooms as the learner continues to become more acquainted with them and more sophisticated about them. In this way children literally grow up in and with their world.

Concept of the Universe:

Seeing the Earth in the context of the universe puts our Earth home into another perspective. This is another step in reaching beyond children's home base. Learning about the stars, the sun, rockets, and everything connected with it is most exciting to children because it helps them form more concepts for their lives' understanding. It also includes adventure, fantasy, and excitement. Many books and materials are available for this, and many schools have units on outer space. This concept can be expanded and built on for older children.

Concept of Origin:

To add to the understanding of our place on this Earth and the here and now, it is necessary to learn something about our origins. Knowing where life comes from forms another basic framework for concept development. Children's emotional need for understanding their own origins expresses itself in their enthusiasm for dinosaurs, cavemen, etc. They want to know the origin of the species and they want to know their own origin. A simple overview of the history of humankind can be developed which would be interesting and understandable for young children. The learning of global history is a normal outgrowth of this.

Sex education is a natural part of the history of humankind. It is necessary for young children. In no other area is their curiosity so great, the information so limited and misconceptions so widespread. How babies are born, why girls are different from boys, the roles of each parent in the creation of a new life, all need to be clarified for them. Children are curious about sex for a number of reasons. Basically, they want to know about it in order to integrate it into their understanding of phenomena in the world. They sense the inhibitions of the parents. Frequently, it is at this point that children learn to live a life unknown to their parents. Sex information should take place either at home or at school and can easily become part of the whole process of education. There is much literature available on this subject.

Concept of Natural Science:

Children are not often given overall concepts in this area. At times they receive information which exists, so to say, in a vacuum. For example, a group of young children was taught the name and characteristics of different breeds of dogs. The children had opportunities to play with the dogs, to learn something about their habits, and seemed interested. However, further observation showed that they had nothing to connect this information with or to build it upon. A number of children did not know the difference between living and inanimate objects, nor did they understand that they were all united under the concept of animals. They were not given the tools to fit the concept of dogs into a unifying structure. A trip to the zoo or farm can serve as an experiential basis to discuss the definition of animals. The ecosystem can easily be taught and demonstrated by examples to young children as part of conceptual framework of natural science.

Concept of Physical Science:

A passage from *Physical Science for Young Children* by Annemarie Roeper and Marian McCloud is appropriate here:

> Phenomena in the field of physical science seemed to hold a special fascination to many children. Why is this the case? The child likes to become acquainted with the world around him. He wants to master it and

understand it, and he likes to be able to depend on his knowledge. Physical science provides a certain dependability that we do not find in nature and in human relationships.

Water always turns into ice in the freezer, ice always melts at temperatures higher than zero degrees Celsius, but Johnny's behavior toward Ricky may be warm one day and cool the next without any obvious reason. Children also enjoy the element of discovery and surprise that is connected with science experiments. A basic concept in the world of science is the three states of matter. Examples of experiments used to present this concept are given in the appendix.

Math Concepts:

Math concepts form part of the building blocks which support the organized image structure built by each child. Math is to be found everywhere in our world. There is much good material available which allows children to discover their own concepts.

Current Events:

Relating events of the day to some of the concepts that have been described above can help children gain some understanding of the confusing bits and pieces of information they are likely to receive in today's world. Without this, confusion often creates a great deal of anxiety. Many children have nightmares or become frightened because of some unexplained information, such as an event they saw on television for which they had no basis to form understandings or opinions and which they did not share with adults. Sharing information with children, giving them explanations, discussing what they have heard or seen with them, gives them a feeling of security and understanding and also provides them with further basis of coping with life and becoming acquainted with the complexities and ethical dilemmas of life. The following is an example of young children's awareness of events.

Example:

When Jack Kennedy was assassinated, many adults were aware and reacted emotionally. The young children realized something was wrong, but did not understand, did not know how to ask, and no one explained. We decided at our school to open the subject of the assassination with the children, although some of the teachers felt we were creating anxiety by sharing the information with them. It turned out that every one of the children had heard. They all had their own version of what had happened, their own emotional and cognitive reaction. One child thought it was his Uncle Jack who had been killed. Some thought it was only on television. They thought Jack Kennedy would get up and be alright when the show was over, because on television you are only half dead when you are shot. Another one identified with the Kennedy children and asked to dictate a letter to Kennedy's son, John-John, telling him that he knew what it was like when your father died, because his father had also died.

The experience gave the children the opportunity to share their feelings, clear up their misconceptions, and participate in a national moment of history and sorrow.

Current events are a part of all of our lives and belong permanently in the classroom. As children grow older, they continue to desire to share feelings and perceptions concerning the daily news. Families who discuss news events over the dinner table develop a larger perspective and a wider world view as well as a basis for ethical conclusions.

Concept of Literature:

Literature is a whole world in itself which becomes a possession of the person who can read and who is passionate about books. A library, the availability of books in the classroom, the opportunity to read, to tell stories and to listen to stories are basic to the SAI concept. This world of books expands as the child grows. Literature and children's reading require a particularly respectful approach. The child's ownership must be recognized. From the beginning, books — rather than readers — can be part of the learning process. Each child has his or her own manner of learning and his or her own interests. The SAI model accepts this and builds on these facts. This facilitates the learning process.

In a community, children like to share their reading experiences and discuss content and reactions. A sensitive teacher will recognize a child's comprehension from such discussions; asking specific questions about a child's ability to comprehend should be avoided. A child who owns his or her reading interprets this as an invasion of privacy. The teaching of reading should be individualized and personal. It does not happen in groups. I consider my own love of reading to be one of my greatest possessions. It is my recreation and my education. Such ownership cannot be mandated; however, the SAI model promotes it.

The teacher is the model, the guide and the facilitator, whose own love of books may transfer to the child. Literature should be prominent all through the school years as it slowly begins to take the form of more formal classes with teachers who share their enthusiasm and their interests with the students.

Concept of Psychology:

Feelings, their existence, their impact, their expression are not part of the traditional curriculum. Therefore, children and adults often believe that feelings are not real, that they should not have a part in our decisions and actions. If a child is sick, we will give him attention, because he needs the care. If a child asks for attention through his behavior, we often look upon it as misbehavior rather than looking at it as just as real as the illness of the child. Children need to understand that feelings and thoughts exist, that they are facts, and that they are also basic concepts. They are part of all human beings and have the greatest impact on our interactions. It is important for children to know that they have a right to feel anything and that everybody has feelings. It is important to help them deal with feelings. It is part of education.

Discussions on the types of feelings shared by all, such as happiness, jealousy, fear, anxiety, anticipation, joy, love, tenderness, etc., are part of the curriculum. For example, one can discuss the difference between love and like. (See Sandra Dooley Lawson's material in Appendix.)

Based on the fact that feelings are real and need to be considered and acted upon, counseling is part of the educational program in the SAI model. It is not to be used only for children labeled as problem children. All children react to some experiences with fear, anxiety, hostility and other feelings which they find difficult to cope with on their own. It should be taken for granted that some adult who is not their parent is available to help children with their emotional reactions to living. Children need opportunities to talk in groups or individually to someone who understands them and supports them. This is a very reassuring factor for the growth of the "Self."

Concept of Daydreaming:

Many, many children daydream. This is seen as a problem in traditional schools. In my consultation service, I have met many gifted children who have been labeled as problems because they daydream in class. Here are a few of the daydreams they have told me about. They dream about how to cure cancer, how to make peace in the world. One child was watching the birds fly south and tried to imagine what it would feel like to know which direction to go by radar. They dream they are princes, they dream they are Superman, they often use beautiful descriptive language to describe their dreams. At that moment, they live in their world of fantasy.

Fantasy is the source of innovation, of discovery. Fantasies may ask the questions which require new answers. Many inventions began with fantasy and led to a new reality. Daydreaming may be the expression of fantasy, of deep thought and feeling. Daydreams require recognition by others as being valuable and valued. Group discussions on day dreams lead to mutual motivation for new projects and inquiries.

One teacher at our school had a bed in her room of four- through six-year-olds. If a child felt a dream coming up, the child could lie down, close his eyes and dream. It was up to the child to decided whether to share the dream with the teacher or the whole group or to keep it to himself. It would be interesting to set time aside for older children to have the option of sharing their daydreams.

Concept of Creative Expression:

Art, music, drama, dance, creative writing, poetry — opportunities for self-expression — pervade every level of the SAI model. They are part of the overall framework. They allow children to feel capable of making an impact on their surroundings and to feel accepted and understood by both adults and children. They enable children to express part of their real "Selves." Opportunities for self-expression exist in every classroom. Naming them all together does not minimize the emphasis on each one and the different importance they have for each child. The arts represent self-expression, beauty, imagination, creativity and coherence. They are integrated into every activity in the SAI model. They are part of the means for the child to make the world his own. Through the arts, the concepts of beauty, imagination, and individual creativity become realized. They are part of the manner in which the individual and the institution find ways to share their essence with parents and others. They are a manifestation of the child's unique "Self."

Concept of Beauty:

Children seem to be born with a sense of beauty. Many children react with delight to a beautiful sunset or pictures or books or music. Opportunities for the enjoyment of beauty are part of the SAI approach. All classrooms are decorated with the children's own art or that of known artists. Music can be heard from every classroom at different times. Instruments are learned if possible. Time is available for enjoyment.

Concept of Play:

Play is never just play. Its place in the curriculum is equal to everything else. It combines fantasy and reality. It offers opportunity for sharing, for leadership, for cooperation, for following. It involves planning, organization, rules and regulations, ethical consideration, physical skills, cognition, and creation. It is a safe arena to try out life, for it is not real life, but mirrors it.

Concept of the Inclusive Curriculum:

Children who are different in their outlook, behavior or interests often feel excluded from the traditional mainstream. The gifted child, the chess player, the daydreamer, the philosopher, the actor, the inventor, the dancer, the musician, the artist, the writer, the storyteller, the photographer, and others need to feel there is a place for them in this world. They need an atmosphere which accepts their individual differences, their interests and their products as valid. An inclusive curriculum allows the child to be free to be him or herself and to express his or her feelings and thoughts. This leads naturally to the desire to communicate individual interests and expertise. The teacher then has the opportunity to know the child's special passions, for these they often are. She accepts them as legitimate and finds ways, if possible, to integrate them into the classroom activities. This can be done through special times set aside for presentations and discussions by the children or become part of organized activities.

Curious Kids Bunch, our Saturday morning program in Oakland, California, has supported an inclusive curriculum as a means of building relationships and fostering the exchange of knowledge, interests and ideas between gifted three- through six-year-old children. As a result, the five year old chess player shared his expertise with classmates while another child added stimulation by bringing a new invention to class every week and a third one shared his enthusiasm for taking machines apart. These became activities that were available to everyone in the classroom.

Concept of Physical Education:

Most people see their bodies as separate from them. They do not know their bodies and do not feel they own them. They use them for transportation, like their car. They judge their bodies and accept them if they fulfill certain conditions of beauty, slenderness or specific physical abilities. Children need to learn to own their bodies, to understand them, to enjoy them, and to see their bodies as part of themselves. Young children should be taught all about the body. It is a field they love to know about. Exercise, different types of dance, movement, swimming, hiking, walking, biking all can help children to become acquainted with their bodies and to enjoy them. Team sports also have a place in the physical education program. The team, of course, is also a community based on competition with others. Competition in the SAI model plays a different role.

COMPETITION AND MOTIVATION:

Competition is a fact of life. Children are competitive. Adults are competitive. There are many competitive situations in life which are unavoidable. Competition does serve as motivation in certain circumstances. However, traditional education is based on competition which incorporates some aspects and types of cooperation, such as team work. SAI is based on cooperation which incorporates some competition. There is a place for competition in sports and games. In the classroom, motivation for learning is not based on winning, but on the drive for mastery and understanding. Children are naturally motivated to experience and incorporate the wonders of the world. The SAI model strives to maintain this sense of wonder. Competition, therefore, is seen as a natural part of living, but is not the motivating force for growth and learning. The child is not taught to see the winning of the competitions of life as the basis for his or her self-esteem.

SKILL LEARNING:

Interwoven into the learning of concepts is the learning of the necessary skills as tools for further concept acquisition. These tools also include a number of additional skills which are not usually considered part of the basic skills. They are the ability to observe, the ability to make decisions and to draw conclusions, the ability to identify with others, and the ability to empathize as well as physical, technical and practical skills. Tools for learning also include all communication skills, among them languages and computer literacy. It is hard to say whether these areas can be defined as skills, but they are some of the tools that make further learning and experiences possible.

In the SAI model, skills are seen as the means to an end and not as the end itself. This creates a different motivation for acquiring them. The child learns to read because it opens new doors, not because of wanting to be the best reader. Acquisition of skills also adds to the child's self-image. He owns his ability to read or to speak a foreign language and can apply it to further learning. SAI does not downgrade skills, but sees them in a different perspective.

Volumes have been written about the learning and teaching of the three basic skills. The debate has gone on for decades. Many have learned the skills well, of course, but among them are those who are conceptual illiterates. I am aware that there is the very real problem of the practical illiterate. I believe this is a problem that must be addressed, but in a different manner. The learning of skills is not relevant to the life skills of many children. The reading material, for example, does not relate to their experiences. For these children also, a conceptual and experiential background which helps them understand who they are will make the learning of skills more natural. The concept, for instance, of likeness among all people of the world as well as their equally valid cultural differences makes the children rightful members of the global family. This, coupled with an atmosphere in which each individual is respected and can make an impact, and where the child can prove himself in areas other than the difficult skill, will provide a positive basis for progressing within these skills.

In the SAI model, teaching methods and expectations are based on the method of learning and the readiness of the individual child. There is much more to be said about the learning and teaching of skills, but this has been done by others and goes beyond the scope of this book.

THE PROCESS OF EDUCATION:

The process of education in the SAI model differs fundamentally from the traditional model in a number of ways. SAI emphasizes learning. The traditional approach emphasizes teaching. In SAI the learner is involved in active acquisition of knowledge, information and learning experiences. The traditional approach is a passive intake of a predetermined sequence of curriculum. Learning in SAI is being done by the individual. Teaching in the traditional model is done to the group. In SAI learning takes place in a large variety of ways through experiences with all senses, the mind, emotions and the whole body. Traditional education teaches to the intellect only. Knowledge is transferred mostly through words spoken, written and read. Emotions are involved only incidentally. There are only a few parts of the body actually involved in traditional learning—the eyes, the ears, and the hands. SAI learning includes opportunities for first-hand experiences, includes opportunities for hands on experiences, for questioning, for exploration, for finding solutions to questions. Traditional teaching is usually second-hand information from textbooks and lectures.

In the SAI model, teachers and students are involved together in the same process. The conscious goals of the teachers and the unconscious one of the children coincide. The goals mentioned above penetrate the daily experiences of children. They may be presented as separate units, they may be overlapping, they may be introduced on incidental occasions. They will be molded by interests and activities and abilities of children. They may be discarded at one time and brought up again at another. They exist as basic goals rather than as a specific, sequential curriculum.

The suggested method of learning, the structure of the classroom procedures and grouping, the role of the teacher are described in the chapter entitled The Roeper City and Country School Experience. I will, therefore, only state here that the method is based on an open classroom approach, on individual education and learning goals, discussions and other group interaction, the inquiry method, experiential learning, an exciting and stimulating learning environment, specialist teachers, homeroom teachers, and a great variety of learning opportunities.

SUMMARY:

In the SAI model, the whole curriculum and learning environment is embedded in and surrounded by a strong interdependent community where the child learns the basic skills and concepts of cooperation. The beginning of the process of education within the SAI model is related to young children and the developmental stage through which they are moving. By the time they enter school, they have established their home as a base and they are reaching out to create a conceptual and experiential context for this home. Some people may be skeptical about the idea of exposing children to so many abstract concepts. I believe abstract concepts actually serve to make experiences more concrete if they are presented in a developmentally appropriate manner. They give the children a reference within which to place their direct experiences. Education must provide direct experiences as well as the conceptualization. It has also been my experience that without such reference children arrive at erroneous conceptions.

These or other basic concepts become the foundation and the framework of all future learning. As children pass through their developmental stages, the curriculum becomes accordingly more complex. It changes in emphasis and moves in many different directions. This may include much traditional material and preparation for college. However, the principle of studying everything in relation to and within the conceptual framework remains the same. This approach by itself will make it necessary to confront the ethical questions involved in the inter-relatedness of everything in our existence. If we study the theory of nuclear energy in isolation we learn the scientific facts. But if we relate it to the environment and study its constructive and destructive uses, we will have to make ethical decisions. Understanding global inter-relatedness raises moral and ethical questions on every level of development.

RULES AND BEHAVIORAL ATTITUDES IN THE SELF-ACTUALIZATION, INTERDEPENDENCE MODEL

This chapter describes the practices and expectations that grow out of the concept of SAI as compared with the traditional hierarchical approach. Many institutions contain aspects of both approaches. Therefore, there will be features of each concept in many families and institutions.

Regardless of the philosophy involved, any human interaction can only function within a mutually accepted framework of communication, interaction, rules, and regulations. The purpose of both approaches is to find ways to safeguard co-existence.

No aspect of life reflects differences of philosophy as vividly and clearly as the manner in which we choose to behave, to regulate and to govern our co-existence. Each system originates from a different belief system, a different mode of thinking. The SAI model represented by the cooperative community, and the traditional model represented by the hierarchical institutions differ in their goals, in their origins, in their contents, in the way one learns to function within them, in the motivation for living within them, and in the way they are regulated or enforced.

DEVELOPMENT:

Both approaches grow out of the family structure, but take a different course.

The helpless child is entirely dependent on the parents. In order to feel safe, the child endows the parents with absolute power and absolute wisdom, which are to be used only for the child's benefit. Parents are allowed no weaknesses, no human frailties, no personal needs, fears or hostilities. There must not be anything that they cannot do. They are responsible for everything. All this is necessary for the very young child who has no social skills and will only feel protected by parents who do.

The traditional family continues this constellation as the child grows. The child learns obedience to the expectations of the powerful parents whether the child feels the demands make sense or not. The authoritarian relationship remains in existence as long as the child is financially and physically dependent on the parents. The child gains independence in such a hierarchical structure only when no longer dependent on the authority figure in any way.

The hierarchical structure repeats the early family constellation, creating a feeling of security and protection. The top of the hierarchy is endowed with all the qualities and characteristics which young children expect of their parents. We also endow the top of the hierarchy with qualities we find missing in ourselves. Because of the hierarchical structure, we never have to develop these qualities.

The hierarchy brings with it certain behavior and defines certain roles for each of us. In the hierarchy, there are those who obey and those who decide. There are those who are in the know and those who are not. Those who are subordinates try to find ways to climb up to the top. They compete with each other. And they increase their power by supporting each other and by developing group loyalty. The top of the hierarchy has the overall power and sets the standard for the other members of the institution. He develops means to enforce them and does the enforcing. The rules, therefore, are designed to support and protect the hierarchy. We build walls around the top of the hierarchy to protect it against others. We defend it against intrusion, because it represents our security.

Adults who have gone through the traditional mode of growing up have to go through a major learning process in order to function in the SAI model. This process entails giving up long-established attitudes, emotions, expectations and skills of a hierarchical approach to life, replacing them with a whole set of new ones. This is an enormously difficult task. It means giving up modes of thinking which are part of our emotional and intellectual inheritance. It means growing beyond dependency on a parent substitute, to accept charge of one's own destiny within an interdependent community. It means allowing one's Self truly to become an adult, to develop one's self-esteem, abilities, skills and knowledge to the extent that we can face the world by ourselves without the protection from someone above. This also means an acceptance of human limitations, an acceptance of the fact that no one can give us absolute security and an acceptance of the certainty of death.

The SAI family belief structure is founded on a concept of cooperation. In this family the standards are based on mutual empathy and realistic needs. The parents are the protectors and models of the child. The goal is for the child to incorporate a sense of responsibility and to react accordingly. The role of the parents changes from taking complete charge to gradually letting the child take over for himself as the child incorporates certain behavioral standards. Thus, parents in the SAI family guide the child toward true adult status. As a child grows in that direction, he begins to dare to see the limitations of parents, to face these limitations as realities, to forgive parents for not being omnipotent, and to learn to face the unknown and the dangers of the world without their protection. Only then can he open his eyes to the fact that the top of the hierarchy consists of fallible human beings and that the Emperor wears no clothes. Only then can he see the fact of interdependence as a reality, understand that a different structure is necessary and begin to consider a possible alternative to the traditional hierarchical structure.

The cooperative community is such an alternative. The community continues to guide the child toward adulthood and self-actualization, as did the parents. In order to become a member of a cooperative community, we must realize that the world is based on interdependence, not dependence or independence; and that, therefore, we need to cooperate. Cooperation is the logical means with which to cope with interdependence. Cooperation means finding solutions which include everyone's point of view. Cooperation means mutual trust, depending on each other. Trusting means openness, no image making or pretense. Openness means sharing of information. Sharing of information means mutual understanding and empathy and finding a common basis on which to make decisions. It means self-actualized, being adult, being able to live with the limitations of our powers, being able to live with the knowledge that we are more protected by cooperation than by a power structure. Understanding the interdependence of cooperation means realizing that all human power is limited. There is no complete protection either in the hierarchy or in the community.

It means understanding that in the cooperative model, hierarchy is replaced by leadership. Leadership is based on expertise, not authority. It is based on the strong helping the weak, on the adult helping the child. It does not carry privilege. It can always be questioned. It is not patronizing.

If we apply the concept of power to the cooperative approach, we can destroy it. If people participate, but do not mean to support it, it cannot work. If, for example, members do not trust the leadership to be truly cooperative, they feel they have to support each other in peer loyalty rather than look at the reality of the situation. Decisions made under such conditions cannot truly be cooperative, for they will not honestly express the needs and desires of the individual members or of the community as a whole. A cooperative approach assures a respect of each person, equal rights, equal responsibility. It also provides a system which does not allow corruption or privilege to develop.

Educating Children for Life   65

All cooperative, interdependent skills are difficult to learn; and it will take some time to trust the system, the leadership and the other members of the community. Since the process is so difficult and there is no clear-cut model, we must learn these skills and attitudes by living them as well as by conscious awareness and interpretations to ourselves and our children.

Cooperative behavior, however, is realistically based on our interdependence. To learn these attitudes becomes more and more important for our global co-existence. Cooperative behavior is like behavior in traffic. Traffic regulations are based on the reality of interdependence. We have learned to live with the rules of traffic, to behave ourselves in relation to others, empathize with the other drivers, to read their behavior, to predict their reactions, to stick to the agreed-upon rules. We realize that if we did not do that, we would be endangering the lives of others as well as ourselves. red light, may not drive on the wrong side, must stay within the speed limits.

DISCIPLINE:

The SAI model changes the concept of discipline from the traditional expectations of obedience to outside rules to the development of an inner sense of responsibility toward ourselves and our surroundings. The actual resulting behavior may be similar in both cases, but originates from a fundamentally different concept. Obedience to rules set by the top of the hierarchy changes to adherence to standards developed from ethical considerations and the specific reality of a situation. These ethical considerations must be shared and understood by all members of the community and accepted as making sense. Behavior and rules may change as situations change. This point of view means that our behavior is actually based on the underlying ethics or other reasons, rather than the rule itself. It may even lead to disobedience of the expected behavior if that behavior is seen as unfair, immoral or impractical in a specific situation.

Example:
Part of our school in Michigan was situated in an old building with narrow corridors. It made sense that running might lead to injury under these circumstances. Therefore, a strict rule of no running was established and was understood by all. On one particular occasion the hall was empty, and one of the boys went running through it. He told a teacher who happened to appear that the hall was

empty, and he was very late for a very important class. This was absolutely acceptable, for it made sense.

Had the circumstances been different, teachers or other students would have reminded him of the rule. If he were to ignore the rule in general, it would mean that he had not developed the necessary inner control or had some emotional reasons for disobeying the generally accepted rule. This kind of behavior would probably be evident upon other occasions. It could be motivated simply by enthusiasm or eagerness or could have some deeper reason.

The reaction to consistent disregard of rules that makes sense is two fold in the SAI model. There are logical consequences to behavior which exist to protect others and the child himself. They are not meant to be, nor are they seen as punishment. In this case the child might have to be reminded not to run, he might be asked to help figure out a way which would make him remember, he might be asked to walk with another student, or he might be asked to wait for the teacher until such time as he seems ready to manage this by himself.

If there are consistent concerns about the child's behavior and reactions, teachers, parents and child look for basic reasons and solutions either together or separately. The problem would be considered from all sides. Why does the child have behavior problems? Is he under stress? Should some change happen at school or at home? Does he not understand the consequences of his behavior? Does he need some counseling? In other words, the emphasis would not be on punishment for disobedience, but on the reality of the child's life situation.

RULES AND REGULATIONS:

In the SAI model, rules are based on equal human rights as well as recognition of differing human needs. The rules are established by the community or, if the rules precede the members, they are explained, discussed and understood as reasonable by those expected to live with them. Rules are always open to question or to reevaluation. Within the SAI model, the young child has the opportunity to learn to internalize a sense of responsibility. The reasons for expectation are explained and the child will learn to adhere to them, not because the teacher says so, but because it makes ethical and practical sense. This is a slow developmental process supported by attitudes, expectations and modeling of the adults. The child will cooperate at first to please the parent or teacher until he learns to incorporate the expectation and takes on the responsibility himself. Slowly behavior becomes motivated by one's conscience rather than by obedience to the law if there is a discrepancy. For example, civil disobedience to racist laws grows out of this concept.

Rules in the traditional model are established by the top of the governing hierarchy and obeyed by the other members of the institution. The rules are not to be questioned. The educational goal is not inner control, but outer obedience. The process of internalization changes. The child does not internalize a sense of responsibility, but the virtue of obedience. This interferes with the growth of the conscience because an outside source becomes responsible for one's actions. In our society, people frequently excuse their criminal acts by the fact that they followed the rules, obeyed the laws, or listened to authority. In this case, the person does not really feel responsible for his or her actions as long as the person adhered to the hierarchy and its rules. The adherence to rules in the traditional system is based on power even though justice and human rights may be the reason for their existence.

Inherent in the rules of the hierarchical model is a concept of privilege for age and status. For example, many schools have a special lounge for teachers where they can be alone or with a group of other teachers. No child may enter this privileged area. This arrangement is explained by the needs of teachers to have opportunity to relax and to be away from the stress of teaching or supervising. This, of course, makes sense and is necessary. However, many children have the same need. They find it a strain to be continually in the company of other children and to function in a group. Children and teachers share the need for a pause, for relaxation. The opportunity for relaxation is not a privilege, but a right equal to all. In a community where equal human rights exist, consideration of teachers' needs does not have priority over consideration of children's needs. The same is true in terms of the needs of teachers. For instance, parents may be in the habit of picking up their children too late in the afternoon, meaning that a teacher may have to stay beyond her allotted time period and neglect her own children. There are many similar examples.

In the traditional hierarchical model, respect for the human being is replaced with respect for authority. For instance, it is not unusual to hear a teacher say in a most impatient voice to a child, "I have told you three times to dot your i's." "Why don't you ever do your homework?" and "You're not listening to me." If, however, the child said to the teacher in the same tone of voice, "I told you three times I didn't understand your directions for the homework," or "You're talking so much I can't figure out what you're trying to say," or "You never call on me," it would be seen as behavior disrespectful to the teacher. The teacher would feel threatened in her authority. In the SAI model both approaches would be seen as disrespectful.

The difference in the two concepts becomes evident in the role of the principal in each model. In the hierarchical model, the child is sent to the principal as a last resort and as the final authority. Along with the child, a great many power messages are sent to the principal in such a situation. It means to the child that he has confronted the teacher's power with his own. The teacher felt powerless to cope with him, which means the child has won the battle. He is now confronted with the superior power of the principal who must take care of the situation with punishment. The child learns about punishment and power, but not about inner control and responsibility.

In the SAI model, the child would not be sent to the principal for punishment for misbehavior, for that indicates that a judgment had already been made. A child would be sent to the principal for evaluation of the situation, to figure out reasons for the problem and ways to keep it from reoccurring. Possibly a change of behavior or in the situation is needed both on the teacher's or the child's part or by the group. Teachers and principals are not beyond judgment. The child may also see the principal voluntarily to receive some help with a dilemma, to straighten out and clarify a problem and put it in realistic form, and also to consider the necessary consequences that grow out of disruptive behavior. It is up to the principal to consider all of the complexities inherent in a situation. The following is an example of how a behavior problem was handled at Roeper School.

Example:

A young girl named Janet was going through a great deal of inner turmoil because of the impending divorce of her parents. At times this expressed itself in very uncontrolled behavior which interfered with class activities. The task was to find a solution to this situation which would help both Janet and the other children in the group.

The situation was carefully discussed with all those involved, the parents, the teacher, Janet, and, to some extent, the other children in the class. It was clear to all, including Janet, that there were times that she simply could not control herself no matter how much she wanted to. It was also clear that this had placed a great burden on the other members of the classroom.

Janet loved the school and wanted to be there. She understood the problem, but was often unable to control her behavior. The parents wanted Janet to be there and so did her classmates and teacher. Also, there was no other school that would have made the effort to help her. The other children became part of the solution, because at no time did they stop letting her know that she was well accepted by them. They really wanted to help.

Finally a cooperative solution was found. On days when her behavior was particularly uncontrolled, Janet would be sent home and would not return until the parents, Janet and the teacher felt she was ready to try again. It was never presented as a punishment, but as a necessary consequence for her behavior. At the same time there was counseling for the whole family and close cooperation between school and home. Janet's classmates understood the cooperative approach to helping those in need. They modeled their behavior after the teacher. They worked cooperatively with the teacher.

As time went on, the situation became more and more stable. Janet's anger diminished and she spent less and less time at home instead of at school. By the end of the school year, the problem had ceased. Janet had been helped to overcome a difficult situation by group cooperation.

During my tenure as Head of the Lower School of Roeper City and Country School, I met once a week for lunch with groups of students from Stage III, aged seven through eight. We used that time to discuss problems and suggestions for their little sub-community. On one occasion the following situation was discussed:

Example:
Many children had a long bus ride to school. A high school student named Bob assisted the school by supervising the children on the bus to assure the safety of the trip. The children had asked me to invite the bus supervisor to attend a particular meeting. Eric had been giving Bob a hard time, had not stayed in his seat, had teased other children, and had reacted very angrily when Bob asked him to follow the self-evident rules of safety which had been very thoroughly discussed and explained.

When this was brought up to Eric, he did not deny any of it. He accepted that he had not followed the rules of safety on the bus, that he was wrong and that he should cooperate and listen to Bob or incur the logical consequence of not being allowed to ride the bus. But Eric wanted his side to be heard also. He felt that Bob did not like him, that Bob picked on him and was unfair for stopping him from doing things others were allowed to do, such as run around. Eric felt that Bob never stopped the older children, only the younger ones. He also said that

Bob had called him stupid which made him very angry. On one occasion when Eric was waving good-by to his friend next door, Bob said to him, "Oh, there goes your dummy friend again."

The group discussed the problem and took it apart into its components. I remained in the background except for reminding them from time to time to let each other talk. The children dealt with these questions in as mature a manner as a group of adults would. One child pointed out that Bob was only doing his duty and that Eric endangered everyone by his behavior. One of the other children said that Eric's behavior certainly was not acceptable, but that it was aggravated by Bob's attitude. They considered the following questions: Should Eric be riding the bus? Should Bob be the one to supervise the situation? Does Bob have the right to call Eric stupid or speak ill of his friend?

During this discussion both Bob and Eric developed an understanding of the dynamics involved and could see each other's frustration. It became clear to all that neither one had reacted with inner control and a real sense of reality. Together the whole group worked out ways to solve the problem and created specific expectations for both of the people involved. It became an important learning situation for the whole group. They realized that one could solve problems cooperatively and that the way to go about it was to put the problem on one side of the table and for everyone to sit on the other rather than to do it in an adversarial manner.

Rules of Trust and Rules of Distrust:

Many rules in the traditional model convey the message that the child's power must be restricted and that the child cannot be trusted. Children must carry a pass when going to the bathroom to make sure they are not out in the hall without authorization or up to no good. A class walks in a line from one room to another, because they might get into trouble if left on their own.

In the SAI model, there are no rules which require children to carry a pass. If they need to leave the room, they may do so without explaining their actions to people they meet outside the room, for it is expected that they are there for a good reason. At Roeper School, children walk on their own from one building to another and are trusted to do so in a responsible manner.

Tattling:

It is logical that the concept of tattling does not exist in the SAI model. It has no place in a cooperative community. However, it is an unspoken rule taken for granted in all traditional structures. It is based on the expectation of peer loyalty. Children are each other's peers and teachers are each other's peers. This loyalty dictates that children do not "tattletale" and that teachers support each other. The peer loyalty supersedes the needs of the community or of the individual. The concept grows out of the power structure which stresses the differences between people rather than their likenesses and separates teachers from children. The concept of tattling is most destructive for children.

Example:

A gifted five-year-old boy whose interests are different from the other children, who speaks differently and does not play like them is teased by a gang of boys. His only way out of this threatening situation is to tell the teacher. The teacher tries to help, but considers the child's request for help as tattling and tells him so. She tries to teach him to solve the problem by himself instead of tattling. The child needs adult support when confronted with an overwhelmingly difficult situation. Many children feel desperately alone when they try to stick to the rule of not tattling which is imposed both by the peer group and the teacher.

In the SAI model the rule of not tattling does not exist. Children communicate with adults as well as with other children. They see themselves as a community rather than a peer group of children separated from a peer group of teachers. There are a number of occasions when it is quite important that children tell a teacher that something is going on. One is a dangerous situation and another is like the one I just described. In that situation the child needs the help of the teacher desperately. The child needs to feel that there is protection and the rest of the group needs to understand that they may not gang up against one child. The teacher's task is to work with the dynamics of the whole group and to try to find out what causes the negative interactions on both sides and to try to help them understand each other and to not allow a power situation to develop.

Lying and stealing are not punished in the SAI model, but instead are confronted and dealt with as the situation requires. Reasons for lying usually go back to fear or defiance and are quite often based on some psychological reason relating to early childhood. Punishment would only justify such motivations. If it becomes a frequent problem for a specific child, it must be seen as a symptom of a more serious problem and needs to be looked at as a psychological and not a behavior problem. A child who steals may do so for a variety of reasons which are also usually psychological ones. The following is an example of how we handled such a situation at Roeper School.

Example:
Money for a class trip had been stolen from the classroom. The children were very angry and upset about this. Nine-year-old Elaine had been seen giving money to other children and was immediately suspected of being the thief. She insisted that she had been given the money by her mother and thought she could do whatever she wanted with it. Elaine was a very unhappy child who craved attention. I was convinced that she had taken the money and explained to her how I could understand her desire to make other people happy, how good it made her feel when they smiled at her. She trusted me based on previous communications we had had and knew I would try to help her straighten this out.

After a long conversation, Elaine broke into tears and finally admitted she had taken the money. She said she wanted to admit it to me from the beginning but did not know what would happen once she told me or what we, together, could do about it. Elaine couldn't face her classmates and did not know how to get the money back. We developed a plan together. She told me the names of the children she had given money and we were able to retrieve it all.

I talked with the class and explained what was happening while Elaine was out of the room. The children had truly developed a sense of empathy. I was amazed at how well they understood and how quickly they forgave her. Elaine's best friend went to get Elaine. When she returned to the classroom, the class took her right in and discussed the situation and how they felt about it. Elaine explained what she had done. Several children asked her not to do it again. It was too upsetting to them.

Such situations are not always solved as easily as this one, but the principle is that they are always seen as problems and not as crimes.

LEARNING INNER CONTROL:

Learning inner control and a sense of responsibility is a process that changes along with the developmental stages the child goes through and involves a number of factors. First and foremost, the child's inner control grows by observing the examples of parents and teachers and from the child's own life experiences. A child who observes and experiences violence and powerplay takes them both as a standard. This child also develops a need to express the anger created by them. The adult as role model is one of the most important factors involved in a child accepting responsibilities as a member of an interdependent group.

Another factor is the interaction among the group of children themselves: the way in which they behave toward each other, the way in which they solve their problems and the way in which they talk about them. This, again, is fostered by the attitudes of the adults. In the interdependent community, the adult takes the time to bring conflicts out into the open, to discuss alternative behavior, to point out the consequences and the chain reaction of behavior and to develop the empathy of understanding the reasons for behavior. In Janet's case, the children observed respectful interaction between adults and children and were invited to share some of the responsibility to help Janet. Participants in the SAI model see themselves as people first and as children or teachers second.

Certain types of behavior do not occur in the SAI model, because there is no realistic need to fight authority or to build up anger against it. There is very little willful destruction of property. There may, on the other hand, be careless disorder, littering and such things that grow out of thoughtlessness. Such situations would be confronted with the students together and rules would be established since no one likes to see a messy campus. I think it might be possible that on a traditional campus the problem of litter would not exist to the same extent because of the acceptance of obedience, but there might be more of a possibility of vandalism because of the accumulated hostility.

THE ROEPER CITY AND COUNTRY SCHOOL EXPERIENCE

ROEPER SCHOOL AS A POSSIBLE MODEL:

In describing the concept which emerged at our school, I am hoping that it might serve as a model to others in developing an approach of their own. I will describe how we developed a non-hierarchical, interdependent model at Roeper City and Country School with the help of the whole community, how we learned by trial and error and how a community concept finally evolved by the time of our retirement. The concept that emerged at our school during our tenure demonstrates the impact created by changes in the educational structure and the subsequent change in the administrative structure.

SETTING:

Roeper City and Country School is situated in beautiful rolling countryside in Bloomfield Hills, Michigan. The school has a campus-type facility consisting of several buildings and playgrounds, with new ones being added as needed. In order to get from one building to another it is often necessary to walk for a few minutes, climb a steep hill, walk through snow and rain. Every part of the environment contributes to the learning milieu. Living with nature and beauty is a constant reminder of the rhythm of life and global interdependence and of our place within it. The landscape around the school becomes an integral part of the program for the whole community. When former students reminisce about their time at Roeper School — the landscapes, walking with a friend, the changing seasons, the beautiful fall colors, the sun shining on the snow, the different type of buildings in which classes are held — are always primary memories.

The school enrolled gifted children from the age of three through high school. There was close cooperation between the school and the surrounding public schools. Many of our students were recommended by public school teachers. The program was based on the philosophy described in previous sections, on the general principles of child development and on the special needs and characteristics of the gifted child. I was in charge of the Lower School; my husband, George, was in charge of the Upper School. Together we ran the whole school.

HISTORY:

The structure and philosophy of the school had its origin in our childhood years and youth spent in Germany in the boarding school run by my parents, Drs. Max and Gertrude Bondy, as well as in the depressing experiences of the early Hitler years. The specific character of our school was formed by our humanistic philosophy, our German-Jewish culture, and our subsequent integration into our new homeland. From my mother, a psychoanalyst, we brought with us the legacy of seeing the emotional development of the child as a major ingredient in the educational process. From my father, an art historian and educator, we gained a sense of community and an emphasis on philosophy, art, and culture. Our interest in the gifted child grew out of our observation that the gifted had become the educationally disadvantaged children in America, and our sense that they might be the ones who would have the capacity to improve the condition of the world someday.

Ours was one of the first integrated schools. We have always been happy about the fact that our school looked like a United Nations in miniature, for its population consisted of children from all different ethnic, cultural, religious, social and economic backgrounds. It was our intention to create a world in miniature, for we believed then, as we do now, that the principles which govern the relationships between the nations of the world are the same as those that exist in a school community.

Originally we began with an approach which was more traditional, though flexible. Children moved from grade to grade, sat at their desks, and followed a regularly prescribed curriculum. However, even at that time, our philosophy was reflected within the framework. Much emphasis was placed on areas other than strictly academic ones, such as music, drama, dancing, current events, and human relations. The developmental phases and the psychology of child development were always included in our perceptions of the child. Our style of leadership at that time, however, was traditional.

As time went on, we became more and more aware of a built-in dichotomy. Much as we tried to focus on the development of the individual child in terms of preparation for all of life, not just for college only, the priority was still oriented toward traditional success. We still expected children to fit into a traditional norm. They were respected for their uniqueness. They had support for their talents. We were concerned with their developmental phases, but if they did not meet the required curriculum, if they did not live up to the norm, they felt they had failed. Somehow they felt their special interest in the environment, for example, did not count as much as learning to spell correctly, because it was needed to master the next year's curriculum. It seemed that personality development and special interests and abilities still remained a low priority.

A feeling began to grow that at our school we had made a promise to children to be allowed to grow unencumbered, but much as we tried, we were unable to fulfill it truly. We wondered why this was the case. We began to suspect that it was caused by the traditional program of the school, which included regular achievement tests and the standard academic expectations. The more we became aware of the characteristics of gifted children, the more we felt that our expectations, which were geared to norms, simply did not accommodate the manner in which these children function. Nor did they include their talents and interests. We began to wonder whether the traditional approach actually met the needs of most children, gifted or not. Even though we could not specify what caused our feelings of disappointment with the priorities that had surfaced, we wondered whether there might be other structures of education which would allow children to develop more freely and would be based on different priorities. We were looking for a system where the child's specific interest, such as ecology or music, would be highly valued, and his problems with spelling would be acknowledged and taken seriously, but not judged as more meaningful than personality development and unique interests.

First we tried an ungraded program where children were grouped according to skill levels, rather than age. This was somewhat more appropriate because it allowed children to grow at their own rate, rather than to follow arbitrary expectations of growth. However, it was still geared to the same goals. Finally, we became acquainted with the English concept of the integrated day and felt that we had found a useful model. After summer workshops with two English experts in the field, we developed and implemented our own specific "open classroom" approach in the early 1970's.

THE OPEN CLASSROOM PROGRAM:

The following is a description of the structure of the Lower School of Roeper City and Country School at the time of my retirement in 1980. Today the school still functions in the same manner in many ways, but I can personally describe only the period during which I served. (Much of the following is from a catalog of Roeper City and Country School.)

The Lower School was divided into three stages housed in a number of different buildings. Stage II consisted of three- to seven-year-olds who occupied five classrooms in a dome building built especially for them. Stage III consisted of seven- to nine-year-olds with four classrooms in their own special building. Stage IV included nine- through twelve-year-olds with six classrooms, all in different buildings. We did not group according to grades or grade level. We developed criteria based on developmental phases, group dynamics, teachers' and children's personalities, interests and a variety of other factors. Therefore, our groups were multi-aged.

Children learn and grow at different rates, and age grouping is not even a correct skill grouping. We do not believe in the lockstep movement of children, since realistically goals and abilities are not equal for all children. Multi-aged grouping took away some of the pressures to move ahead and to compete, which then could be replaced with motivation through interest and learning for learning's sake. It also allowed for a much more flexible placement procedure, for a child could be placed in one of five groups rather than in one of two. This approach made it possible for children who developed differently in areas of skill and socialization to function in an environment which filled both of these needs.

Example:

A four-year-old child who read on a first grade level, or even beyond, but played and functioned like other four-year-olds would find in the four- through six-year-old group both the child who played as he did as well as the child who read as he did. He did not have to feel misplaced as a four-year-old in a first grade due to his social behavior or feel a lack of learning opportunities in a four-year-old group.

We found that ages were practically forgotten and older ceased to be considered better, nor did it become an embarrassment when an older child found that a younger child had certain skills that he did not yet have. Multi-aged groups increased the opportunities for a child to live in a group in which he felt comfortable, well-integrated and appropriate. In case that still was not the case for a particular child, that child could be regrouped, even after the beginning of the year, after careful discussion between parent, child and teachers.

In our model teachers were seen as human beings who had their strengths and weaknesses, not as the experts whose task it was to teach the passive learner so that he could keep up with the rest of the class. At times the specific characteristics of the teacher could be either helpful or disadvantageous for a child. Parents who learned to see teachers as people with individual characteristics and needs would express their criticism of the teacher's approach in a more humanistic manner. Everyone realized that parents, children and teachers were involved in a common process of growth and support. In this context, a mismatch was not failure, but realistic and human. A teacher could be more free to admit that another person might be better equipped to help a particular child grow and learn. However, this was never easy.

As head of the school, I often facilitated meetings between parents and teachers. Surprisingly, in many cases it became a sort of growth process for the adults to learn to admit weaknesses without feeling ashamed and to learn to cope with problems in a comfortable and more realistic way. The process became cooperative rather than adversarial. It did not always succeed. But even failure can be seen as understandable human interaction in this context.

THE ROLE OF THE TEACHER:

The specific role of the teacher has been described in a previous chapter. They became guides, protectors, experts, counselors, facilitators and bridge builders in addition to teachers. The teachers were usually called by their first names and children felt free to disagree with them. Since they were seen as human beings, teachers could freely admit mistakes without losing face. This was particularly important because it was possible that a gifted child would have knowledge in a certain field that the teacher lacked. This never minimized the leadership role of the teacher as long as she was a truly capable, knowledgeable, and enthusiastic person and saw herself also as a learner who was committed to the child.

Each homeroom contained about 22 children. There were assistant teachers, full-time for Stage II and part-time for Stages III and IV. The homeroom was based on an open concept. There was an overall flexible framework of curriculum expectations which built the bridge between the child and the world. This surrounded the child's freedom to grow in his own way according to his own timing and to follow his own interests. Teachers organized their own rooms in whatever manner seemed to be most natural to them. We felt that our diversity of teaching styles was one of our assets and made it more possible to match the specific need of a child with the specific strength of a teacher.

The homeroom teacher was concerned with the child's growth in language arts, math and social studies, integrating it into the growth of the total unique child. The role of the homeroom teacher also included that of a counselor for each child. The teacher kept all the threads together that related to the entire life of a child within the school and how the school related to home. Under his or her leadership the teacher and the group created the learning environment within the classroom, in which the children were academically, physically and emotionally involved.

Children need personal attention and group interaction, therefore, we created opportunities for teachers to work with children individually, in small groups, or in large groups. Children need to experience successful results. They need help to plan and follow through. Therefore, we created different ways to allow all this to happen.

An awareness on the part of the teacher is required to know each of the children well, to know their individual range of interests, skills, and commitments. Therefore, individual meetings between teacher and child, the writing of journals, work on individual schedules and keeping careful track of each child's work became an integral component of the program. Children need a teacher to whom they feel a sense of belonging, even though they may not spend all day with him or her. Therefore, a personal relationship was stressed. Teacher and child learned to know each other well and often felt special to each other. This support also expressed itself at times through the teacher's insistence that commitments be kept or behavior controlled.

There are times when children want the adult to help them to do something they cannot bring themselves to do, but need and want to do. I would like to emphasize this part, because many people confuse the concept of the open classroom with the concept of permissiveness. The question is not discipline or permissiveness, but the reason for an adult demand. Are demands based on the child's needs or the interest and needs of the institution, the teacher or the parent? In our model the decision and the manner in which requests were carried out were based on the needs and personality of the child.

Therefore, for example, we did not put pressure on a child to learn to read by the end of first grade simply because this was a traditional requirement; but we did insist that a child learn to read whenever the child seemed ready and basically willing and desirous, but could not overcome a certain resistance. On the other hand, we would help a three- or four-year-old to learn to read if the child was interested and ready. A child's learning style and the trust between teacher and child were the basis on which such demands were made.

In addition, some general requirements are necessary to make it possible for the child to cope with her present environment. The teacher needs to consider the child's reality and help her to cope with it in a way that will support the "Self" rather than restrict it. Therefore an outer framework of realistic expectations and rules is created surrounding the inner freedom for growth.

The philosophy as well as the personality of each teacher and the children in the class were expressed in the physical arrangements in the classroom. From the classroom arrangement designed for group learning, we changed to an arrangement for individual learning and groupings. From a physical framework for passive intake of information, we changed to active involvement in the incorporation of information. From emphasis on academic skills only, we moved to include social skills, skills of cooperation and a specific interest, such as photography. Desks and assigned seats were usually replaced by strategically placed tables of different sizes and shapes, sofas and other furniture inviting children to move around, to interact, to work together. Instead of everything being directed toward the front and the teachers, many different centers of interest were arranged.

THE ROLE OF THE SPECIAL TEACHER:

In the SAI model, all areas of learning and stimulation are of equal importance. Therefore, equal emphasis was put on creativity, physical exercise, and unusual types of academics as well as the traditional areas. This led to an extensive system of special teachers who offered a variety of subjects for even the youngest child. There were many different aspects of music, art, drama, dance, French, and at times, Spanish, all areas of science, human relations and areas of temporary interests. Even very young children need to develop a feeling of power over their destiny and to learn the skills to use this power wisely. Therefore, children need to develop the skills to make appropriate and meaningful choices and also to have the opportunity to grow and to learn in their specific areas of interests. To fulfill these objectives, time and expertise were needed which went beyond the framework of the homeroom. Therefore, the following program evolved.

A number of the special teacher program classes was mandatory to acquaint the children with all the different areas of experiences that were available to them. Great emphasis, however, was on a whole network of electives. Stage II had a free choice period every morning when they could go to any one of the special teachers and subjects they chose. It could be music, art, library, science, physical education and occasional others.

In Stage III, commitments became more long term and complex. Each child could chose several of the classes offered. A special class for this Stage usually met for six weeks on a once or twice a week basis. The choices of Stage IV were even larger. As many as eleven classes were available for them. Sometimes this included choices of different classes in the same subject area. They might be able to choose between singing and recorder in the area of music, or between chemistry and electricity in science.

The special teacher program added a great deal to the richness of the learning environment by offering a number of additional experiences. A child could pursue a special interest in greater depth. A child had an opportunity to build a relationship with someone other than the homeroom teacher, someone who shared an interest and had a special expertise in the area in which the child wanted to grow. Children had the opportunity to work with children from other groups who also shared their specific interest. They developed sophisticated skills in making decisions. This ability is needed in our modern life situation when one is confronted with choices on a daily basis.

Parents also needed to learn to allow children to make their own choices, even when they thought the children made a choice contrary to their own wishes. The parents needed to realize that this was part of a learning process. Homeroom teachers and parents learned to help children think through their choices and make their own schedules. This approach also showed children that they were capable of participating in their own destiny and that adults trusted them to make choices and to go on their own to their special classes, even if the special class met in a different building.

The special teacher program had other benefits as well. At times during the day there would be a small number of children in the homeroom, because the rest were in special classes. This gave the teacher the opportunity to have individual conferences or to concentrate on some special work with particular children. Homeroom teachers and special teachers were in constant communication about each child. The special teacher often had insights unavailable to the homeroom teacher because the special teacher would be able to follow a child through as many as six years of growth and development.

THE DOMES:

The center of the Lower School program became the Martin Luther King Domes. Stage II was housed in them. All Stages ate in them and had special classes and activities in them. They were designed in a cooperative effort by the architects, the school community and the wider community. Every member of the school, small children as well as teachers, the dietician, the school nurse and others, expressed their opinions and needs concerning space. The children did this through papier mache buildings. The adults' ideas were collected in a small book. All of this was at the disposal of the architects.

In addition, a symposium was held consisting of a number of architects, members of the educational community of the Detroit Metropolitan Area and representatives from local, state and federal government who were concerned with educational facilities. The architects listened to the thoughts and guidelines of the educational community and then submitted a number of proposals. The result was a unique building made out of styrofoam which fulfilled many, although not all, of the hopes and expectations of the school community.

The domes were designed in a manner which tried to implement the school's philosophy and to facilitate it. There were spaces for individuals, spaces for small groups, spaces for homeroom groups and a space for the entire school. There were spaces for special classes and special activities as well as assemblies, lunches and physical education. There was space for privacy as well as togetherness. The building allowed for a natural flow rather than regimentation. It also created some problems, especially acoustical, and required that teachers learn to function within round rooms instead of the rectangles they were used to.

In addition to the administrative offices, there were two very large domes. One of them was a multipurpose room used for lunch, physical education, dancing, assembly, performances, etc. The other was called the academic dome. It was divided into four pie shapes which contained the library, science, art and math rooms. However, over the years, some of the walls were knocked out and they were used for different purposes. Six smaller domes were attached to the two large ones.

STAGE II:

The smaller domes became the classrooms for Stage II. They were the home base of security for the children. Each homeroom had a teacher and an assistant. Each room reflected the special interest of the teacher and the development level and interests of the children in the group. Each small dome was equipped with a good deal of space for storage and exhibits. One room might reflect the teacher's special interest in science through the types of exhibits and books all around the room. Others leaned more toward math, reading, social studies, art or music. All teachers were concerned with each individual's uniqueness as well as with the individual growth in academic areas.

At this Stage in particular, play is a serious factor in growth and learning, therefore open and ample time was made available for it. The domes were designed in such a manner that the areas around them divided themselves naturally into different playgrounds. These were well equipped and offered more opportunity for play. From the security of the home base, children learned to venture out further into the building. It was at this level that the program of special classes and free choice began. It was interesting to observe how the children's ability to make decisions matured. At first they would venture out into the academic dome only in the company of a good friend, while later on they were proud of their independence and were able to make their decisions on the basis of a particular interest.

A typical day began with a meeting in each classroom where everyone talked about experiences, made plans, and discussed various topics. In some cases a theme might grow out of those discussions, such as: What is the difference between day and night? That theme might then pervade all the activities of the day or week or month in one form or another. This period would be followed with a work period or a special project for some and outdoor play for others. It might be a planned period or a free time. This would be followed by free choice and special classes. Usually, for reasons of space, half the class would leave the room while the other half remained to do individual academic work, have special time with the teacher, or whatever might be indicated. This might be followed by a story time or, sometimes, silent reading. Then came lunch in the large dome followed by a rest period for the youngest. For others this might be time for a special project in an academic area such as social studies. The day would end with more outdoor play.

Once a week an assembly for the whole Stage took place. They would listen to music, sing, see a performance, or have a whole group discussion. There were frequent walks and trips, usually related to specific projects.

STAGE III:

As the children grew older and became more independent they moved to Stage III where a greater amount of commitment was expected. They occupied a small building of their own, with four homerooms. The homeroom continued to be the base of operations but the children could go further afield physically. Since we had a campus-type set-up with many buildings, some special classes might be up in the main building, in the Stage IV buildings or in the Domes. The children all came over to the Domes for lunch, but went to the special classes on their own without a teacher. This allowed for an unusual measure of independence. The children rarely abused this trust.

The homeroom teacher in Stage III was still a support and guide for the expanded commitment expected from each child in terms of his or her developmental growth. This was demonstrated by the children's long- or short-range projects and by their signing up for special classes which ran for several weeks or the whole year.

The Stage III morning began with a meeting in each homeroom. Announcements were made, plans and changes in schedules were discussed. This was followed by a period with reading, writing, math, social studies, special projects, etc. Expectations were different for each child. Some work was individual; some was group oriented. Each of the four homerooms was self-contained. Within each room a great number of activities usually went on at the same time. Several children might be in the math corner working together on the math lab. Others might be writing a report together or stretched out companionably on the rug reading. The teacher moved around the room making suggestions, presenting new materials, helping a group decide how to present the facts learned from interviewing the Upper School staff the previous week. Five people might work in a small room with the French teacher and, in a note chalked on the blackboard, a boy could inform his teachers that he had gone outside for a few moments to give himself some time away from an irritating friend. There might also be activities and programs involving the whole group.

STAGE IV:

Five homerooms were the base of operations for mixed age groups of nine-, ten-, eleven- and some twelve-year-olds, with about 22 children in each room. Along with the five homeroom teachers, Stage IV had a full-time science teacher. The part-time special teachers included music, French, Spanish, art dance, physical education, drama, and library.

Each of the five homerooms provided a rich learning environment encompassing many interest areas devoted to skill building and individual and group discovery. The children moved freely around the room working on activities geared to their special needs and periodically leaving to meet with other groups in accordance with each individual schedule.

The students made their own schedule. It was an eleven week commitment, made with the help of the homeroom teacher and, at times, parents. At the end of each eleven week period they could elect to continue a special subject or try a new one.

Some classes were held in buildings other than the three Court Buildings and the children were responsible for getting themselves from one class to another. The homeroom system provided the secure home base for the children and allowed the homeroom teacher to work closely with students he or she knew well. There were cohesive group activities for extended projects and opportunities for developing personal responsibility toward oneself and others.

At this level children had learned many basic skills as well as developed an understanding and acceptance of their own uniqueness. They began to set some goals for themselves, began to have a serious and knowledgeable interest in world affairs or specific areas of research and learning. Discussions became more sophisticated, along with their feelings and thought processes. They were more able to do independent work. They were also at an age when physical changes began to take place, which also led to a different interaction and needed a different type of leadership from the adults. Teachers tried to incorporate all of this new development carefully and sensitively in the program and group interaction. At this age more speakers were invited to assemblies and more places were being visited within the framework of sophisticated projects. Plays, musical performances and dance continued to play an important role in this Stage. Overall, their world expanded from the safety of the classroom and school to the world beyond, just as Stage II children moved from their classroom to the building and activities beyond.

Each homeroom group started the day with a meeting. The plans for the day might be shared and group and community problems discussed. The homeroom teacher explained the daily assignment which might include language arts, social studies and math, not necessarily as separate subjects, since all learning overlaps. Some might be done at the end of the day, some later in the week. There might be a notice asking certain children to meet at a special time to hold a math lesson or a play rehearsal. Plays might be written by children, stimulated by a social studies project, and incorporate in them art activities as well as music and dance.

After the meeting everyone went about his or her own business. Some might leave the room for a while and go to another of the Court Buildings for science, drama, typing, French or Spanish, Black History, newspaper, Women in Society or special math, etc. Others might go to the Upper School building for art, music, recorder, or other instruments, or to the Domes for dancing or trampoline, or outdoors for physical education. The children remaining in the room worked on their assignments alone or in small groups, seeking the teacher's help when necessary and going to the library whenever they needed particular books or information.

The atmosphere was one of comfortable, cheerful, companionable activity. Small groups formed, dissolved, re-formed according to the present need. Everyone knew what was to be accomplished and learned quickly, in the process of doing so, how best to get tasks done. The teacher became more and more of a facilitator as the initiative shifted to the children. Decision-making and responsibility for one's own actions were perhaps the most important skills learned. When a child was disturbing others, it was more effective to have it brought to his attention by the children who were being disturbed. Everyone learned through this process. Human interaction is a special thread which weaves through each day, knitting and knotting, breaking and being mended between all ages, until everyone is aware of what effect his or her words and actions have on other human beings.

STUDENT GOVERNMENT:

In Stages III and IV the children participated in decisions of their community. Once a week I ate lunch with representatives from each group. We discussed their concerns and their suggestions. They then took the resolutions back to their classroom or an assembly. Out of this, many student-initiated projects grew, such as: the annual "overnight" at school, building new playground equipment, campaigns against the use of swear words, protecting endangered species and many other areas of concern and interest. Students often had new and creative ideas and worked diligently to implement them and were given the opportunity to do so. They learned to cope with the complexities of community life and see that their input was valued and that they could make an impact.

The majority of the students moved from Stage IV into the Upper School where the program changed according to the developmental phases and the individual needs of the children, but continued with the same philosophy and basic principles. From there they graduated to college and a career. We hope they had developed a strong self-image which allowed them to feel secure and creative in themselves and the world.

COOPERATION AMONG TEACHERS:

The teachers in each Stage worked as a team. They were in charge of governing the Stage. All areas were coordinated by a Stage Coordinator. This job often rotated and might be held by anyone, teacher, assistant, or special teacher. The Stage Coordinator was not seen as a department head in a hierarchy. In their weekly meetings, teams of teachers planned the program for each unit in all respects. They set up rules, guidelines and procedures. They concerned themselves with the issues of the moment. This could be academic procedures, racial awareness, sex education, relationships between younger and older students, or concerns that were related to the needs of the teachers or the school. Each Stage was semi-autonomous and had a structure based on their particular children's developmental needs. The interaction between Stages took place in monthly teachers meetings or the Administrative Council.

Homeroom and special teachers met regularly to discuss each child's development. Children could be moved at any time from one room to another or from one stage to another after consultation with the child and parents. Differences of teaching styles and emphases were openly discussed and were used as a criteria for original placement or change. The child who had behavior problems in one environment often found a ready-made, comfortable niche in another. There were several meetings with the parents during the year, often with the child included, and a written report which was handled differently in each stage was sent out once a year. At the end of each year careful placement was made by the entire group of teachers. The child could remain in the same group for one, two or three years, move to another group within the same Stage or move to a new Stage.

STUDENT EVALUATION AND PARENT COMMUNICATION:

As we made the change to the open classroom, standardized tests became less and less applicable. However, children, parents, and teachers needed some kind of guidelines as to how the child was developing academically. This was not in terms of keeping up with others, but rather to have knowledge of how the child was feeling and functioning. Much was discernable by work samples and projects collected by the teacher. We gave diagnostic tests in certain areas and used parts of achievement tests when we felt they were useful for a particular situation. We never taught to a test, never greatly emphasized testing, never competed with other schools in this regard, and never did any class ranking. Tests were used to the extent to which they helped the parent, child and teacher to understand the past and to plan for the future.

There were two official conferences with parents and many spontaneous contacts at school or over the telephone. Both parents and teachers communicated with each other freely. In addition to this, two descriptive reports were sent to parents about the growth of the child. This included the different individual areas, such as social, emotional, creative, academic, and physical, as well as the overall development and the uniqueness of the particular child. The children often wrote self-evaluations or participated in the conferences. The school report was often addressed to them as well as to their parents.

GOVERNMENTAL AND ADMINISTRATIVE STRUCTURES:

The role of administration is crucial in any educational endeavor. The governmental and administrative structure have an enormous impact on the school community or educational institution. Therefore, it is critical to discuss how they evolved at the school in relationship to the self-actualization philosophy and the educational program.

As the children became more and more able to participate in their destiny, the dichotomy between the system of education and the system of administration became evident. While the children functioned within a cooperative model, the adults worked within a hierarchy. It was obvious that the adult community, teachers and support staff needed to be able to participate in the same manner in their destiny at school as the children. Many of us realized that the structure of administration was not in keeping with the philosophy of the school. We felt a fundamental change was needed. It became our mandate to fulfill this need and as we did so, all of us together, we entered uncharted territory with no model to follow.

We began to look critically at the whole structure. How can the best decisions be made? Can they be made in a hierarchy? The head of the school has the overview of the institution, deals with all sections of the community: children, parents, teachers, support staff, finances, physical plant, superintendents, etc. The head does not, however, share the experience of individual teachers in their individual classrooms, or the experience of the lunch supervisor in the dining room, or the bus driver driving a bus filled with children on icy streets. The school's overall functioning depends as much on all of these individuals as it does on the head of the school. These individuals do not have an overview of the school on which their situation depends. They depend on the head to have that, just as the head of the school depends on the behavior of all of these individuals.

If everyone's experiences are shared and mutually respected, a truly better decision can be made than if it is only made on the top and the others have to fit into it. The sharing of information, experiences and decisions creates an awareness of their mutual interdependence and how to live in it. As these thoughts became more and more formulated in all of our minds and in those of the staff, we began to make some basic changes in our structure.

We actually dismantled the hierarchy. The evolving structure that replaced the hierarchy was called "participatory democracy" or sometimes, "flattened hierarchy." A type of hierarchy still continued because of the existing board structure under which the school operated. My husband and I, as the Heads of the school, had final decision making power within the school.

However, we were able to develop a new participatory process within this existing governmental framework. Most importantly, we all learned to think in nonhierarchical terms. It became more and more clear that the process which led to a decision was as important as the decision which was finally made. The participatory approach was based on the principle that everyone who would be affected by a decision would have the opportunity to be involved in the process which led to the final decision. The initiation of this participatory process created changes that affected every aspect of the school community and every individual, including the Board of Trustees.

The Board decided that one student, one alumnus, and two people chosen from the whole community, which included teaching staff and support staff would become voting members of the Board of Trustees. The staff members and the students were appointed by the Board from a selection of two or three people elected by the staff.

Within the school there were many different ways in which the staff participated on a more regular basis in planning and decision making. The center of the administrative structure was formed by the Administrative Councils, one for the lower school and one for the upper. These two groups met periodically in a combined meeting. In the lower school the Administrative Council consisted of the administrators and coordinators of each stage and anybody else who was interested in attending these meetings. Those who would be affected by a decision to be made at a given session were likely to come. Areas discussed would vary from curriculum planning, interaction of different subjects, to playground supervision or teacher sabbaticals. Anything that concerned the community could be brought to the Administrative Council by anyone who wanted to. Everybody present participated in the discussion and decisions.

We formed a Benefits Committee which consisted of teaching staff, support staff, and administration. All matters of staff concerns, such as salary, sick-leaves, medical insurance, etc., were discussed and either sent as a proposal to the Board, or were referred to other internal committees if more appropriate or if not solved by the Benefits Committee itself. This is the exact opposite method of conflict resolution from the one used in unionized concerns; our focus was on cooperation, where those are based on confrontation.

The staff also participated in staff hiring, evaluation, firing, enrollment and many other areas. Some of these areas I would like to describe in greater detail so that the difference from the traditional methods will become more evident.

HIRING:

Hiring of new staff members was done through group interviews after I had selected four or five suitable candidates from their applications, telephone conversations and references. Staff members from the Stage which needed a new teacher—as well as staff members from the Stages before and after and special teachers—signed up to participate in the evaluation procedure. Knowledge of our expectations in terms of philosophy, ability to teach, ability to relate to peers and children, expertise in subject matter, were common goals of all who participated. The staff had the opportunity to watch the candidates teach, to read the applications and to participate in an evaluation session when the staff and the candidates would all try to get acquainted with each other. The candidates usually spent additional time in the school talking informally to different people. Each person would ask questions of the candidate from his or her own perspective and gain his or her own impressions.

From all of these experiences, a decision would be reached. As a rule, we arrived at a consensus. Sometimes a vote was needed. Often strong battles ensued, but people were usually able to express feelings rather than letting them fester and interfere with their personal relationships.

Even though the final decision making rested with me, I practically always accepted the recommendations which we had reached together. There were a number of occasions when I might not have reached the same conclusion by myself, but I had a deep belief in the process as well as in the fact that groups of people make better decisions than individuals. A precondition for this is that there must not be any hidden, personal agendas, such as helping a friend or wanting to gain power. At times, however, we all made mistakes together; but in that case the process and the responsibility for those mistakes were shared by all. Our hiring process usually resulted in efforts by all concerned to help the new person find a comfortable place in the school community.

TEACHER EVALUATION:

One of the participatory areas of our self-actualization, interdependence model was teacher evaluation. Traditionally a head evaluates a teacher and determines hiring, rehiring, or even firing by a formal or informal process. These decisions are based on the administrator's personal observations with possible input from a division or department head, through informal input by other teachers or pressure from parents. We discontinued this completely. Instead we developed a committee with a very careful evaluation procedure.

A special committee worked on this for a long time with input from the rest of the community. Therefore, members of the community believed in the process, which included a self-evaluation and a committee of other teachers, administrators and assistant teachers. One of these was chosen by me, one by the evaluee, and two additional volunteers. In the case of a specialty, such as music, outside experts might be invited. It also included specification on the amount of classroom observation by each evaluator. A little booklet was designed which outlined the questions to be asked and the areas to be observed. There were also formal and informal discussions between the person to be evaluated and the members of the committee. After all this material was collected, the committee met, created a written document which I then discussed with the person evaluated.

These evaluations often led to surprising insights, and the original casual perception may have turned out to be untrue. Through the structure, the perceptions of less outspoken members of the community became known; the most vocal people are not always the majority. Thus evaluations became more fair by representing a broader range of viewpoints and more accurate information.

The evaluation process was perhaps the most difficult change that was introduced at our school and required a large degree of openmindedness and objectivity as well as capacity on the part of staff members to be more objective. Once the process had been decided upon by everybody, the need for peer loyalty no longer existed and was replaced by loyalty to everyone in the community. Peer loyalty grows out of the common experience of dependency on the hierarchy above. This new kind of loyalty which is really a loyalty to basic human rights could only happen through the trust that grew in all members in the community and through the evaluation structure. It was most difficult, however, to change these basic attitudes which were so deeply ingrained in all of us. There were many times when all of us would relapse into former concepts which would then make it difficult to carry out our newer purposes.

As a whole, this structure created more openness and was more acceptable to the person being evaluated than previous methods. Even though dismissal and criticism always create anger and disappointment, they seemed to be more acceptable through our participatory method. Most people developed a new sense of security, knowing that decisions would be based on broader and fairer evaluations. And if a staff member was asked to leave after a very careful evaluation, it would not create a sense of insecurity as easily in the others who otherwise might wonder if they would be next.

ENROLLMENT AND PLACEMENT:

Teachers also participated in the enrollment process which evolved over the years. It was important that the child fit into our specific environment and that the parents agreed with our approach to education. Each child visited a classroom for a day. The parents filled out a lengthy questionnaire and had a personal interview with the Head or another administrator, not as a screening device, but only as additional information to be considered.

An evaluation morning followed the individual visits. It was usually on a Saturday morning. All of the applicants were seen by different teachers, homeroom teachers as well as special teachers. Each teacher would spend some time with each child talking about any subject that seemed important, helping write papers, doing some math work, doing a painting or some exercises. We did not use regular tests, but developed our own themes and methods to find out whether a child could do well in our particular environment. At the same time an administrator would speak with the parents as a group to become more acquainted with them and to help them become more familiar with the school.

All the information on whether placing a particular child in our school would be appropriate was gathered and considered by the evaluating teachers right after the evaluation morning concluded. Objective as well as subjective information was used as a basis for the decision. The responsibility for accepting a child was shared by all. This meant that teachers had made a commitment to a child from the beginning, rather than having had no choice in the matter. There were many cases, when teachers decided to accept a child with problems because they felt the desire to help him. Often they succeeded. Had they just been confronted with the child, they might have resented it and not become as involved in supporting the child.

RELATIONSHIP WITH PARENTS:

The atmosphere of openness also brought about a subtle change in the relationship between the parents and the school. Many parents always saw themselves as part of the community and participated cooperatively. However, certain attitudes now became official policy. Since teachers were no longer seen as teachers only, but as human beings as well, it was acceptable if they did not succeed with every child. The parents felt freer in expressing their concerns and these were discussed openly.

In the past parents who had a criticism about a particular teacher would want me to rectify it but did not want to be identified to the teacher. Nothing is more disturbing and less helpful than being told by an administrator that people are critical of you when you do not even know the context and the background from which this concern has evolved. We insisted that people take responsibility for their perceptions. I often functioned as a facilitator in disagreements between parents and teachers. It was interesting to see how parents developed techniques to be honest without hostility and how teachers became secure enough to cope with those instances without becoming threatened or afraid.

THE ROLE OF THE ADMINISTRATOR:

Our administrative role changed from being the top of the hierarchy to becoming the facilitators of the group processes. We saw ourselves as responsible for the new process of education as well as the new process of administration. We saw our area of expertise as the overview of the school while each staff member was the expert in his or her area of experience. Information from all these areas would be combined to make decisions.

Decisions which were made together were owned by all. This meant that all were responsible for the results. It took a while before this stage was reached emotionally by everyone. There was a period when if a common decision resulted in a failure, it was still felt by the group that the administration alone was responsible. From this point, however, the group moved on to a general acceptance of responsibility for the decisions in which they participated. An important by-product of the procedure was that the debate took place before implementation. In a hierarchy, the staff would be confronted with a "fait accomplis" and, therefore could express their concerns only after a decision has been made. This often leads to so much pressure that the administration has to change its mind in retrospect. In our case, the debate and constructive discussions took place before the decision, thus avoiding and often eliminating the period of discontent altogether.

Children and adults developed a new sense of freedom and found it easier to express their differences openly. All of this required very deep inner changes in the way we saw our mutual relationships and interactions. It was difficult, even frightening, for some of the staff to understand that the heads of the school did not have the power to provide absolute security and would not accept responsibility for everything. We all had to learn that chances for security are greater when everyone works together openly.

For some it was difficult to give up the concept of seeing us as parents and to replace this with a concept of us as friends, facilitators, and experts in the overall administration of the school. There were also practical problems involved. The new process was very time consuming to develop and difficult to organize. It took a while before we learned which areas entailed major decisions and which had only to do with organizational factors and did not require a group process. Overall people needed to accept the fact that no groups within the community had priority over others when it became a question of their human rights. This was hard to understand, because the reason for the school's existence was the education of gifted children and the adults were there to fulfill this purpose. Within this framework however, decisions had to be made based on a philosophy of equality; for only if there is no hierarchy of justice can children be ultimately safe.

By the time of our retirement we felt that our new structure had come of age, that we had achieved an administrative structure which expressed our philosophy. We knew that it was not perfect, that human interaction is never smooth, often painful and often unjust, no matter how hard one may try. But we felt also that human reactions are not only influenced by their personal attitudes, but also by the structure in which they function.

We saw the cooperative structure as circles within circles, overlapping circles, as opposed to the pyramid of hierarchy. The child or teacher is the inner circle with the classroom surrounding them, overlapping with special classes and other classrooms. These structures, in turn, are surrounded by the stage system and the lower school or upper school, and then the entire school and Board. These again are surrounded by the community, country, and the world. It was our hope that children who grow up in an atmosphere of equal human rights will have the same perception of people in the world.

FINAL THOUGHTS

There are many other ways in which a community based on a concept of self-actualization and interdependence can structure itself. No matter how it is designed, it can only function when its members learn to live within it. Attempts at creating such structures have been made many times in history and often they ended in failure. The failure does not make the concept invalid. It only means people have not learned to function within it. Wherever we look, we see the cooperative spirit among the peoples of the world. However, our organizational structures and lack of skills in cooperative living often stand in the way. We have developed the emotional reactions and the skills of functioning in a hierarchy over hundreds of years, while our ability to function in a community of interdependence has not been expanded. Much of living in such a community expresses itself in the way it is experienced and the atmosphere in which it occurs.

We can acquire skills and attitudes of cooperative living only by living them. We believe that education for self-actualization and interdependence is the basic curriculum for modern life. In our school we endeavored to create a structure which allowed these skills and attitudes to grow.

APPENDIX

SOCIAL STUDIES

The following curriculum was used by Annemarie Roeper with young children at the Roeper School.

THE EARTH

Begin with an introduction of the globe as a model of the Earth. Introduce the concept of models in general, how they differ from the real object, how they provide certain advantages to us. There is only one earth, but endless globes. Pictures are like models. Pictures look like things, but are not the things themselves. Have the children bring pictures of themselves and ask them, "Which one is you?" Return to the globe. Ask why people do not fall off the earth. Put magnetized figures on a metal globe. Discuss magnetism and demonstrate it in different ways. Then introduce the concept of gravity. Have the children reach up with their arms and see how long they can keep their arms up. The children will realize that gravity pulls them down. Discuss other aspects of gravity. Can you see, smell, taste or touch it? What would happen if gravity did not exist?

Discuss what lives on Earth, what Earth looks like, going on in an open-ended manner. Follow this with a discussion of countries, of people living on different sides of the Earth. Interesting details such as people in China are getting up as we are going to bed can be discussed. This can lead to a discussion of how people in the United States and China are alike and how they are different. Children may look different and have different habits and ways of doing things, but all children grow up, need to eat and sleep, need to be taken care of, have feelings, etc. One can then study different countries, read stories about them, show movies.

All of this can serve as an overview for more indepth future learning.

PHYSICAL SCIENCE

The following excerpt is taken from a science unit presented in *Physical Science for Young Children, A Guide for the Teacher* by Annemarie Roeper and Marian McLeod.

THE THREE STATES OF MATTER:

The chapter on the physical characteristics of matter served as a tool for better science understanding in the young preschooler. In that chapter the young preschooler experimented with the words and uncovered more fields to explore. The inquiry of the peer group varied to a degree, but there were certain areas of paramount interest to all. In order to facilitate understanding, another set of tools can be introduced. As all physical phenomena are roughly evidenced in one of the three states of matter, this is an easy frame work in which to work and explore. This concept is quickly grasped, as a classification is given to the child about what he has observed and sensed in the difference in material and make-up of his environment. It defines and supplies a name. It draws a distinct difference between his meat and milk, his bath water and soap. He finds great excitement in the commonplace.

Exercise 6

Purpose:
To discover that a solid has a definite shape and has mass

Materials Needed:

wooden block	scissors]	brick
stone	pencil	nut
rock	chalk	paper
stick	book	orange
whistle	apple	spoon
doll	candle	soap

Experiment:
Place all articles in a large paper sack. Bring out one at a time and pass around having each child examine the article. Encourage the children to look, smell, touch, taste, and then listen to the article. Each article should

be named. Ask the children how they know it is a stone. Ask them how they know this is an apple. Then play a game. Ask a child to close his eyes and identify the solid you have placed in his hands. How does he know that solid is an orange? By taste, touch or smell? When the children are all familiar with the articles, ask them how these things are all alike. In what way is a rock like a brick? A bar of soap like a candle? Help them to discover in this manner that all these objects are solids because they are hard or have substance, have mass—heavy, and a definite shape. Use the word solid over and over again. A solid possesses certain identifiable physical characteristics which distinguish it from a liquid or gas.

Exercise 11

Purpose:
To identify the physical characteristics of liquids.

Materials Needed:
Each child needs a paper cup containing a small amount of
    one of the following:

water	antiseptic	fruit juice
cooking oil	milk	ketchup
detergent	vinegar	

different solids
pail or plastic container (min. 1 gal. capacity)

Experiment:
Have children sit in a circle with container in middle. Pass a few cups around and have children identify contents. Hand each child a cup containing a liquid. What is in the cup? One at a time, have each child pour some or all of the contents of the cup into the plastic container. Have children shake or stir the container. Ask them if they can take out the liquid they put in. Always refer to the contents of each cup as a liquid. Repeat several times. Keep asking what happened to the milk, water, etc. Where did it go?

Give each child a solid. Have them identify and place it in the container. Have them shake or stir contents. Ask them if they can pick up their solid. Why? Repeat as necessary.

Pour a liquid on the table or floor. Try to pour a solid. Splash the liquid with your hand. Have children do this. Try to splash a solid. Discuss which splashes and which pours. Why doesn't the solid splash and pour?

The identification of a liquid by its physical characteristics:
1. Assumes shape of container
2. Pours
3. Splashes

Exercise 14

Purpose:
Solubility.

Materials Needed:
popsicle sticks for stirring
eight paper cups 1/2 full water
the following solids:

salt	corks	flour
powered paint	sand	sugar
stones	wood bits	

Experiment:
Have the children try to dissolve the solids in the liquids. Have many helpings in small amounts, so that they do not super-saturate the liquid immediately. Allow them to add all of the different solids to the same cup of water if they choose. Each child can have a cup of water or a large vessel of water may serve the whole group with everyone adding to it. While the children are experimenting, it is important to ask what is disappearing and where it is going. Have the children name the materials that disappeared—DISSOLVED. Where did they go? Discuss other things that "dissolve" in water. What things can they put in water that seem to disappear? Do these materials really disappear? Where are these solids?

Exercise 17

Purpose:
Detecting the presence of air.

Materials Needed:
paper cups
cork
straws

large container of water
small glass

Experiment:
1. Give each child a straw and have him blow bubbles in the water.
    What are those bubbles?
    Where do they come from?
2. Puncture a hole in bottom of paper cup.
    Ask what is in the cup. Can they see it?
    Invert and immerse in water.
    Where are bubbles coming from?
    Repeat until air is identified.
3. Float cork in water.
    Hold up small glass and ask what is in it. Can it be seen?
    Invert over cork and immerse.
    Where is the cork going?
    Why? What is pushing it down?
    Repeat as necessary.

MATERIAL DEVELOPED BY SANDRA DOOLEY LAWSON

Sandra Dooley Lawson, a teacher for nineteen years at Roeper City and Country School, developed the following topics for four- to six-year-olds in order to help them develop their unique "Selves" and express themselves. She learned these topics from interacting with the children.

1. WHO AM I? - Identifying a special facet of me.

2. MY HOME, MY FAMILY - Looking at steps from home to a larger world.

3. SOMETIMES I'M AFRAID OF THE DARK, DARK, NIGHT - I am not alone in my fears; others have them.

4. MY IMAGINARY FRIEND - I can create and understand the things I need.

5. SOUNDS AND SENSES - Listen and look so you can learn everything that goes on before you.

6. BRIDGES AND WALLS - Reach out and extend yourself to others.

7. IF I COULD STEP UPON THE STAGE, I KNOW WHAT I WOULD BE - Looking to the future.

8. BLACK AND WHITE - Finding the light and darkness in all of us.

9. THE FEELING ME - Learning to be in the moment with your feelings.

10. GIVING BIRTH TO NEW IDEAS - An awareness of constantly changing and recreating your world.

For each topic, Sandra Lawson developed an appropriate framework within which the children felt comfortable expressing their feelings by means of acting, dancing, singing, talking, story telling, etc. For example, with topic number seven she built a little stage, let each child dress up in available dressup clothes, and step up on the stage as he or she said, "If I could step upon the stage, I know what I would be," followed by talking or acting out how his or her future would be. She also took photographs of the children and gave them an opportunity to react to them. The fact that this was a pretend acting situation made it less risky to tap their unconscious, inner "Selves". Some of the children surprised us enormously with their versions of life, growth, and the future and their own creative as well as tentative or jubilant approach to it.

ROEPER WEST SCHOOL

Roeper West School (RWS) opened its doors on September 5, 1989. Even though it has been in existence only a short time, the school has a long history. Roeper West School is based on the philosophy and programs of Roeper City and Country School in Bloomfield Hills, Michigan, which was founded by George and Annemarie Roeper in 1941. Roeper City and Country School is one of the foremost schools for gifted and creative children in the country. It was one of the first independent schools for gifted children and, with its school population of about 500 students from age three through high school, has become a model for many private and public schools throughout the country. Annemarie Roeper, Ed.D., is a co-founder and educational consultant to Roeper West School.

Roeper West School is dedicated to meeting the educational, emotional, social and physical needs of creative and gifted children. Its educational philosophy is rooted in a new understanding of the modern world and a vision of global awareness and interdependence. The school emphasizes the process of learning as it grows out of each child's developmental progress and the growth of the "self." Our educational philosophy is based on the discovery and nurturing of each child's individual ways of learning, rather than primarily on the teacher's ways of teaching.

Roeper West School is located near UC Berkeley, two blocks northeast of the intersection of Euclid and Cedar. The school has at present two large classrooms and two offices in the Hillside School building, with a third classroom to be added in the fall of 1990. There is a large playground with play equipment and space for a variety of sports activities.

Roeper West School does not discriminate on the basis of race, creed, gender, national, or ethnic origin, in either its admission policies, educational programs, or hiring practices.

PHILOSOPHY

Our philosophy of education is also a philosophy for life. We do not limit our goals to education for college or for entering the professions or the work force; we are concerned with the whole impact of life on the child and the impact that he or she will have on society. Roeper West School believes in a commitment to actions based on justice rather than on power. This begins with a willingness to allow the student to participate in the shaping of her/his own destiny, beginning with her/his own education.

Roeper West School seeks to create an educational environment in which each child can develop fully as an individual and also as a participant in society and in a world of global interdependence. We believe that quality education for creative and gifted children should address the whole child, not just those areas that are most visible or easily tested. Importance is given not only to academic areas, but also to creativity and imagination, social, emotional, ethical and physical growth.

WHOM ARE WE EDUCATING?

Gifted and creative children experience the world and go through their developmental phases differently than other children. From the beginning, they are more aware of the complexities of this world. They are bombarded with a multitude of impressions and have an enormous desire to make sense of it all. Their great awareness may lead them to develop different coping mechanisms. Thus, giftedness in young children expresses itself as much in the processes through which they go, as in the products which they create.

Creative and gifted children often have a tendency to feel like outsiders. Being with others like themselves allows them to feel comfortable and to see themselves more realistically. These children have a well-developed sense of justice and may bring up ethical questions pertaining to any subject. It is also characteristic of creative and gifted children that they have an enormously wide variety of interests and expertise. These include many areas beyond the emphases of traditional education.

Creative and gifted children display a great deal of curiosity about many things and a striking intellectual playfulness. They approach materials and ideas through fantasizing, playing with images, and trying to elaborate on and improve existing institutions, objects and systems. They are also characterized by a keen sense of humor and often see humor in situations that may not appear humorous to others.

THE PROCESS OF EDUCATION

The traditional definition of learning is the intellectual acquisition of material through information to be absorbed, problems to be solved and skills to be mastered. This approach is cognitive only. Our definition of learning, on the other hand, is the integration of material into the student's life. Integration takes place through all the senses. It combines intellectual, emotional and physical mastery, including, but going far beyond cognitive mastery. The emphasis is on learning rather than teaching.

Our educational programs grow out of:

* The overall philosophy and goals of RWS for our students: the growth of the individual student and her/his integration into the larger society.

* The psychological, intellectual, creative and physical characteristics and developmental phases of children in general and creative and gifted children in particular.

* A belief in the ethic of responsible involvement in the world.

The School Community

One of our basic concepts is that of community. Therefore, our school community is at the center of the learning process. A school community is in many ways a replica of the world and the institutions in it. The models of conflict resolution learned by the students in the school community are applicable to all levels of conflict in society. Our global awareness approach introduces students to the interdependence of individual and communal issues.

Class Groupings and Size

Our classes are non-graded (multi-aged) for a number of reasons. Some gifted children have difficulties with certain areas of skill learning such as spelling, handwriting and even reading, although a great majority soon become avid readers. Creative and gifted children do not all develop at the same rate, and are often very determined to follow their own interests in learning. Therefore, a mix of ages often leads to a better match in ability levels and interests.

Another reason for the non-graded classes is that creative and gifted children, more than others, function at different learning levels simultaneously. Thus, a 7 year-old may be a non-reader but know all about electricity, rockets and outer space, while a 5 year-old may be reading at a 4th grade level but needs the play environment appropriate for her/his age group.

Creative and gifted children benefit from intensive interaction with teachers and stimulation to help them find answers to their questions and to process the abundance of information and experiences they take in. In order to provide for these needs, classes at RWS are small. Children may be regrouped in the course of the day to accommodate interests and ability levels.

The Role of the Teacher

The role of the teacher at RWS is not the traditional one. The teacher is a guide, a model and a provider of a framework of expectations within which a child can develop her/his own ways of learning. The teachers also provide a cooperative model of school administration, incorporating into the running of the school the RWS ideals of interdependence, and shared responsibility.

Creative and gifted students are often extremely knowledgeable in certain areas to the extent that a homeroom teacher alone cannot offer sufficient breadth of expertise to help them progress in all areas. For this reason, specialist teachers are employed in different subject areas. As experts in a field, be it art, science, or history, they bring excitement and love for what they do, along with a greater depth of knowledge, to the students.

CURRICULUM

The RWS curriculum differs each year and for each student, therefore, the following description of the curriculum addresses general underlying principles. There is an emphasis on global awareness through themes such as evolution and heredity, environmental concerns, science and math concepts, as well as social studies and an understanding of human relations. The creative areas of art, drama, music and creative writing have an equal emphasis with the basic skill areas of the curriculum.

Traditional basic skills are mastered through concept learning as well as separately, according to individual needs. Teachers work frequently with small groups and individual students. Using learning centers, students can individually control the depth and breadth of learning and rate of progress in each subject.

Within our individualized learning model there is a basic framework of expectations for each student in terms of skills to be acquired, and concepts and materials to be covered. This framework serves as a bridge to the traditional curricular requirements, so that a child can move comfortably back into the mainstream at any time.

Daily life at home and at the school is seen as an integral part of the curriculum since a school community has the same dynamics as any world institution which creates the major events shaping our world. Children participate in the functioning of the school by means of regular school meetings in small groups with the director and/or the teachers to discuss suggestions and concerns about the life of the school. Their concerns are then taken up and acted upon in a school assembly. This enables the children to experience first hand the dynamics and struggles which make up human relations, social institutions and political processes.

Any given subject is not taught as a compilation of facts, but as a set of complex intellectual structures which build one upon another. Once concepts are grasped, the details become more meaningful and provide further illumination of the overall ideas.

GENERAL INFORMATION

Roeper West School is a non-profit organization governed by a board of directors including some of the original founders, parents, and teachers, experts in the field of gifted education and community leaders committed to the RWS philosophy of education. The school sees the education of a child as a triangle of child-school-parents, and works very closely with parents. The school office is always open for parents to get information and bring their concerns. Two regularly scheduled parent-teacher meetings are held each year and a written report on each student's progress is made at the end of the year. There are additional meetings and informal discussions between parents and teachers, as the need arises.

For the school year 1990-91, RWS is expecting to have three classes aged approximately 5-6, 7-8, and 9-11 with a total of 45 students in the school.

School hours are 9:00 AM to 3:00 PM every day but Wednesday, when school ends at 2:00 PM to allow for staff meetings and planning. Students may arrive at the school at 8:45 AM. After-school care is arranged by separate contract and is available 3:00 PM (2:00 PM on Wednesdays) to 6:00 PM.

ADMISSION POLICY AND PROCEDURE

Roeper West School seeks to enroll children who will flourish in an environment designed to enhance creativity, imagination and individual gifts. Diversity among all members of the school community is valued. RWS does not discriminate on the basis of race, creed, gender, national or ethnic origin in the administration of its educational policies, admissions and hiring policies, scholarships, or any school related programs.

Our approach to the admission process is based on the concept that creativity and giftedness express themselves in many ways: cognitively, affectively, and artistically. It is our goal to get a sense of the whole, unique personality of the child. We do this by "experiencing" the child through information from the parents and school and through the observations of experienced staff members.

We do not impose any expectations on the children during the observation, but rather allow them to be themselves. We learn about them through the clues that they give us and attempt to understand and appreciate their strengths and weaknesses based on many years of experience with creative and gifted children. A more extensive assessment will be used as indicated. When appropriate, information from the child's previous school will be requested.

The admission process begins with submitting a completed application form and questionnaire to the Roeper West School office at 1581 LeRoy Ave, Berkeley, CA 94708. This is followed by a parent visit to observe the school and meet with the Director. Then a visit will be arranged for the child to spend about an hour at the school, interacting with the students and the staff. Finally, the school staff reviews all the available information and contacts the parents to inform them of the decision.

Please call the school at (415) 849-4207 for further information and to request an application form.

ROEPER WEST SCHOOL STAFF

The Director, Beverly Goodloe-Kaplan, Ph.D., University of Pennsylvania, holds a Creative Problem Solving Institute Certificate from SUNY Buffalo, New York. She has been on the Executive Board of the Northern California Council for the Gifted and the World Council for the Gifted. An author, international teacher, consultant, and lecturer, all of her professional work has been on behalf of gifted and creative children.

"As Director of Roeper West School, effective March 1990, allow me to share my hopes that our school will join the original Roeper School in Michigan as one of the foremost schools in the country for gifted and creative children. Our whole-person approach, one of the most significant tools in our program, allows us to address the educational, emotional, social and physical needs of these children.

My commitment is to offer leadership that enhances the quality of our program while encouraging the diversity of talent among our staff. Our child-centered, developmental curriculum includes an emphasis on fostering social responsibility and global awareness in an open classroom setting. Student groupings are small and formed on the basis of individual potential and academic progress. Our teachers and subject area specialists work together to insure that the high expectations we hold for our program are met in a flexible but systematic manner."

Annemarie Roeper, Ed.D., is a co-founder of and educational consultant to RWS. She was the co-founder and co-director of Roeper City and Country School in Bloomfield, Michigan, established in 1941. Dr. Roeper is co-editor of Roeper Review, a journal devoted to the education of the gifted. She is a lecturer, author of numerous articles and of the recent book <u>Educating Children for Life: The Modern Learning Community</u>.

Anne Beneventi who teaches the lower class has a degree in Elementary Education and Special Education. She has helped found and has been a teacher at independent schools in New Mexico and Egypt. More recently, she has taught gifted children at the Nueva School in Hillsborough, California, and for the Curious Kids Bunch program in the East Bay.

Anne's goal of teaching through the use of themes based on the childrens' interests, integrates all subject areas. She incorporates storytelling and puppetry to transmit factual information and to guide moral development in a non-judgemental way. She strives to foster a positive self concept and a joy of learning in her students.

Pat Petty teaches the middle group (ages 7-8). She holds a B.A. degree in Public Administration and City Planning from University of Florida and a California State Multi-Subject Teaching Credential earned at Chapman College. For the past ten years Pat has taught environmental education, story telling, puppetry and drama in the Bay Area. She has combined her interests in teaching, environmental education and children's drama by writing and producing with children several plays including a screen play, "Yosemite," to be released in conjunction with the Yosemite National Park Centennial celebration in Fall 1990. Pat has recently taught gifted and talented children in the Richmond Unified School District.

"My approach to education emphasizes integrating subjects into a creative curriculum that fosters self-discovery though hands-on problem solving and builds self-esteem and environmental awareness."

Bessie Citrin teaches the older class. She received a BA in Human Ecology and a Teaching Credential with specialities in conservation education and minority perspectives from UC Berkeley. She has taught at both public and private schools in grades K-8. She is also a math teaching consultant conducting teacher training, workshops and demonstration teaching for schools throughout Northern California.

Bessie holds a Masters degree in clinical psychology from the Wright Institute in Berkeley, and is currently completing a Ph.D. in this field.

Bessie's work is based on a recognition of the immense powers of each child as a learner. The classroom environment provides an opportunity for each child's independent investigation as well as challenges and activities selected by the teacher. As students mature, development of self-disciplined learning and production is encouraged. Children question and challenge as they develop their own tolerance for criticism with themselves, other students and adults, and become increasingly articulate and self-assured.